The Extraordinary Life of an Ordinary Man

A MEMOIR

PUBLISHED BOOKS BY THE AUTHOR

Secular

How to Use Leverage to Make Money in Local Real Estate

How Real Estate Fortunes Are Made

George Bockl on Real Estate Investment

Recycling Real Estate: The Number One Way
to Make Money in the 1980s

Spiritual

God Beyond Religion

Living Beyond Success

Where Did We Come From and Where Are We Going?

(being offered to publishers)

A Conversation With a New Thinking Sage

The Extraordinary Life of an Ordinary Man

A MEMOIR

*with special emphasis on
how to elevate
real estate development
into a
spiritual enterprise*

GEORGE BOCKL

Christy Company Publications
Milwaukee, Wisconsin

The Extraordinary Life of an Ordinary Man

ISBN: 0-9741403-0-9
Library of Congress Catalog Card Number Pending

FIRST EDITION 2003

Christy Company Publishing
321 N. 121st Street
Milwaukee, Wisconsin 53226

Printed in the United States of America

Dedicated to

MY MOTHER
whose bravery gave me a life in America

Table of Contents

—— PART ONE ——
LIFE IN RUSSIA

—— PART TWO ——
MY LIFE IN AMERICA

Part

1

Life in Russia

Chapter 1

My Grandfather's Blessing

I'm 93 years old with a gift for remembering the events that shaped and defined my life. I witnessed the turbulent Russian Revolution, and after that there were the challenges in America when I arrived at age 12. I have two perspectives in writing: from the standpoint of a child, and from my present perspective.

My remembrance begins at age four, sitting alongside my white-bearded grandfather on a horse-drawn wagon filled with barrels of beer that he was delivering to various homes and businesses in Bobruysk, a city of about 150,000. My mother would take me to the barn early in the morning, where I would watch my grandfather hitch the horse to the wagon. I got to like the smell of horse manure because it was part of the routine of spending a joyous day with my grandfather.

We had a lot to talk about because I had a lot of questions and my grandfather had a lot of patience. As we rumbled across streets that kept on changing from cobblestone to sand, I kept up a steady patter. Why are horses stronger than people? Why is there such a stench when we pass the city dump? "Because," grandfather answered, "city workers collect the drek (human feces) from peoples' outhouses and dump them there. And as much as I don't like to drive past it, there is no other way to get to where I have to deliver some barrels of beer."

When I was about five years old he told me that my father was in America; and when I was six and seven he explained that my father left for America to earn money for several years and then would return to live with my mother and me in Bobruysk.

(I was an only child.) "But a big war stopped him from coming back," he said, "and now your mother is planning to leave Bobruysk and join your father in America."

"I'll never go without you," I remember blurting out.

"But I'm too old to go with you."

"Then I won't go either."

Riding alongside my grandfather, and occasionally holding the reins, were the best memories of my childhood. He was my father, my mother, my rabbi, no one could replace him.

He was illiterate, but the wisdom of the Ten Commandments shaped his morals and his gentle view of life. I liked the way he explained them much more than the way the rabbi did, with whom my mother insisted I spend an hour a week – against my will, because I didn't like him.

The love between us grew at both ends. He was my security, my daily adventure, a patient listener on whom I poured my babbling childish questioning that meant so much to me. I knew he enjoyed my companionship because he was as much interested in my lively blabber as I was in his thoughtful responses. I loved him so much that I felt lonely when he joined my mother and a cousin with their grown children in conversation during evenings.

When I was eight years old, my grandfather stopped work and in a few weeks he was bedridden with some disease. I hovered over him, still asking questions, but his answers were weak and apathetic. One evening he called me to his bedside and, putting his hands on my head, blessed me. A half hour later he died. I cried all night. He took part of my life with him.

My life changed drastically. My mother's sister with her five children – two younger and three older than I – lived a peasant's life in the tiny village of Sitskeveh, about 10 miles from Bobruysk. With my grandfather's earnings gone, my mother decided to trade Bobruysk items like cloth, kettles, ribbons, etc.

with the Sitskeveh peasants' potatoes, eggs, milk, etc., and sell the food to Bobruysk dwellers.

I spent the next two summers in Sitskeveh and gradually began to turn my security toward my mother and my aunt and her children. Sitskeveh was a one-road hamlet with about 20 farms on each side of a narrow dirt road. Their land extended to the edge of thick forest on four sides. One edge of the narrow road led to Bobruysk.

My Jewish aunt, whose husband left for America at the same time my father did (and for the same reason) was tolerated by her peasant neighbors, but not liked. Her children managed to get along with the village children, but up to a point. The point was the religious divide.

During my first summer in Sitskeveh, life was not only peaceful but enjoyable. I drank a glass of warm milk within min-utes after it came out of my aunt's cow, a delicacy I cherished every time it was offered to me. Once a week I would join my aunt's family, with empty kettles in our hands, to go picking mushrooms and wild raspberries at the edge of the forest. This was the time when we talked about Rassulkas who lived deep in the forest, half human and half animal – women who, we were told, occasionally snatched infants from parents to live with them in the depths of the forest.

The only discomfort I felt physically, living in Sitskeveh, was that because the small house was crowded with children, I had to sleep on top of a five by ten, five-foot high brick oven in the cen-ter of a large room that was used for cooking, baking, and heating the house. Small cloth-partitioned bedrooms surrounded the oven. My nose was always dry from the brick dust and warm air the brick exuded during the night from the day's cooking. Worse than that discomfort was that, for some reason, a huge 14-year-old boy would sneak up behind me and scream "Sbuhal" (I scare you) and burst into guffaws of laughter when he saw me jump with fright. His fun was my misery, and there was nothing I or anyone else could do about it. I was on the lookout for him, but so was he for me. He won so many times that it marred my otherwise pleasant farm life.

But the hurricane cloud of the 1917 Revolution had moved into the second summer of my stay in Sitskeveh. Polish soldiers had occupied Bobruysk and they spilled over into Sitskeveh. They drafted all able bodied men and women to dig trenches, my aunt among them. They robbed the peasants of food, and raped some of the women. We could see their cannons at the end of the road, and the soldiers mingling close by. Gone were the halcyon days of last summer. Instead we were on constant alert with fearful expectations. I was nine years old, developed enough to feel the tension in the air.

My mother, anxious for my safety, was staying with her sister to be near me. Her fears were realized when one evening there was some unusual clatter and commotion among the soldiers which my mother surmised was in preparation to leave for Bobruysk for the rumored battle between the Bolsheviks and Poles who were occupying the city. She feared what the Poles might do before they left. My mother called me aside and said, "Gershen [my Jewish name], we're leaving for home early in the morning."

It was not early enough. As we were hurrying on the road to Bobruysk, we heard the grinding of wheels faintly behind us, and it was getting louder as we lurched into a trot. "I can't run anymore," my mother puffed, "I have to slow into a walk." After a half hour, when we began hearing the neighing of horses, we began running again. I had no problem, but my mother was near collapse. I took her hand and, breaking into a fast walk, we finally reached the outskirts of Bobruysk. We reached our house after traversing a few deserted streets, and my mother collapsed into a heap at the door. I pounded on the door, and the relatives who lived with us carried my mother into the house.

The rumor of the impending battle became a reality. As we lay on the floor, we heard an occasional boom of a cannon, the crackling of gun shots, faint voices, and the clatter of feet when they were near enough to be heard. Now and then we were startled by a whining bullet as it pierced our flimsy roof. Our fears rose when we heard prowlers' voices at our next-door neighbor's house. Soon we heard a woman scream, then a gun shot followed by silence. We waited. The assailants walked away.

After waiting a harrowing hour, Jankev, who with his wife Merke and their four children shared my mother's house, said emphatically, "I think we'll be safer nudging ourselves against the rear of the barn than remaining here." Stealthily we crossed the yard, entered the barn, and pushed aside several vertical boards. We squeezed through and moved the boards back into place.

It was pitch black. We hugged the damp earth against the outside boards. The rear of the barn faced a huge apple orchard. I clung to my mother, and every time I heard running, screaming and silence, I shuddered and moved a notch closer to her.

Late in the night, my fears were diverted from what was happening out there in the orchard by footsteps in our yard, and then voices in the barn. They were saying something in Polish, and my heart pounded with anticipation. They stayed a few minutes and from what I figured, looked into my grandfather's wagon and then slowly walked away. When light broke in the morning, we went back to the house.

Soon we heard people yelling and cheering as a rag-tag army of soldiers passed by, marching and celebrating the Bolshevik victory. We came out of the house and happily cheered along.

Chapter 2

The Revolution Crashes Into My Community

W hen I was 10 years old, Marx's ideals and Lenin's practical ideas moved in on me directly, enveloping me in 'the midst of the storm. I didn't understand their theories, but I felt the harsh applications, even though I kept hearing their ideal, "from each according to his ability, and to each according to his need." Communism became the god and was forced on the masses. From my present vantage point of understanding, I can see why it succeeded: zealous nobodies were given a chance to become somebodies; thugs and ne'er-do-wells were given managerial positions; and intellectual pundits who had no place in Czarist culture became commandants and commissars.

It was happening all around us. The 20-year-old Vladimir, son of one of the peasants in Sitskeveh, and the derelict of his large family, became the leader of a communist contingent to collect cattle from the farmers to feed the growing Bolshevik army. My aunt told me that when Vladimir, with two soldiers at his side, stopped at his father's farm and demanded two of his cows, the old man snarled, "Get out of here! You were always a good-for-nothing and you still are. Your uniform doesn't change a thing." Vladimir got off his horse and, with drawn revolver, walked up to his father. "There's a bullet here for you if you don't get out of the way," he said. He motioned to his soldiers, "Pin him while I hitch the cows to the wagons." While the father ranted, Vladimir commandeered part of the cattle from the rest of the Sitskeveh peasants and drove away. He was rumored to have killed others who vigorously opposed handing over what they had worked for all their lives to survive.

A shoe-factory owner in Bobruysk shared the same fate the peasants did, but his loss was total. Three armed soldiers walked into the shop and announced what the owner had feared and what the workers had hoped: "We're taking over the factory in the name of the communist government. From now on you'll be working for Russia instead of Sergei Baranovich." The workers cheered approval as Sergei walked over to the leader and asked, "What happens to me?"

"Because you were wise in not offering opposition, we'll make you one of the workers, but if we see any sign of counter communism, we'll kill you."

One of the factory workers told this story to Yankev, who lived with us. Other businessmen who resisted were either sent to Siberia or killed.

Alongside the initiatory steps of taking the cattle and produce of small farmers and usurping owners' factories or businesses, the communist apparatus formed the Komsomols, where they indoctrinated youngsters from about 11 years and up with the glorious ideal of communism. My friend Berul was among them. His father was a mean man and they often quarreled. On one occasion, the father blasphemed communism, and when Berul vigorously defended it, his father beat him up. One of the important doctrinal commandments Berul was ordered to practice was to inform on anti-communists. With fervent patriotism, he told his leader how his father hated communism. Based on the son's testimony, the father was sent to Siberia.

"How could you do this?" I chided Berul after the incident made the rounds.

"Communism is more important than an ignorant parent," he shot back, "and I'd advise you to be careful how you talk to me about communism."

The newly formed committees dealt more drastically with large land owners, the Kulaks, than with the small peasant farmers.

The Hlusha estate, with several thousand acres and hundreds of workers, was about 15 miles from Bobruysk. What happened there was told to Yankev in our home by one of the workers. Three armed soldiers drove up the knoll where the large mansion overlooked the estate and ordered Tomash, the owner, to call his workers together to listen to the written message which was thrust into his hands. He read it and angrily burst out, "I'll never do it!" One of the soldiers stuck the barrel of his revolver into Tomash's mouth and snarled, "Read it, or we'll kill you and we'll read it." Tomash weakly nodded his head. After several hundred Hlusha peasants gathered in front of the mansion, Tomash began to read: "Fellow workers, I've lorded over you for many years, always looking out for what's best for me, not for you. From this day on there will be a change. I'll be working alongside you for a new Russia dedicated for the welfare of all people, not for the selfish luxuries of the Czar. You and I are entering a new age, all for one, and one for all."

The Hlusha takeover went off smoothly, but from what I heard elders discuss, many neighboring ones ended in bloody confrontations.

The transition periods between Czarism and communism provided a heyday for robbers and anarchists. The Jews in Bobruysk suffered from rampant plunder, as well as from pogrom gangs. The absence of law and order flushed out criminally inclined men who cared neither for Czarism or communism, but only indulged their demented minds. Yankev's grown sons, David, Motte, and Gregory, offered some protection, but Yankev had the good sense to offer free food and lodging to Pretor, a Gentile friend, who was a good, kindly man, and who offered us Christian protection. We were fortunate not to be robbed or massacred in a pogrom, but when my mother and I visited Sitskeveh on one occasion, we were not so fortunate.

Toward evening a huge man with a musket flung over his shoulder filled most of the doorway and in a coarse menacing voice said, "I want 100 rubles or I'll kill all of you." His bovine, lifeless, deranged look threw us into great fright.

"We're poor," my aunt said in a quivering voice.

"Then I'll kill you," the bandit said matter-of-factly. The children let out a wail of cries, I among them. It did not stop him from slowly lifting his gun off his shoulder, and as he leveled the gun at us, my mother leaped forward and in a trembling voice begged, "Wait! Between my sister and me we'll scrape up the 100 rubles for you."

"I'll wait," and he put his rifle vertically alongside him while the two women whispered, and then went to a rear cloth partitioned room. They came out with 100 rubles in their hands. He took it and without a word walked out of the house.

From what I heard at the discussion table between Yankev, Pretor, and other elders, the "Reds," as I heard them refer to communists, were wiping out all resistance from the "Whites," the remnants of Czarist supporters. The Kerensky name popped up during the discussions. He was described as an advocate of a milder form of communism, but he soon was pushed aside by Lenin. Stories of killings by plundering bandits increased in the neighboring villages of Shelibe, Krevoya and Zhlobin. I heard that the Red government itself was beginning to commit atrocities against the Kulaks and what was left of the Czarist hierarchy. Things were getting progressively worse.

My mother was an illiterate, feisty, brave woman, with a lot of innate common sense. One evening when we were alone, she put her arm around me, and what she said put my mind in a whirl. "Your aunt and I have decided to escape into Poland and then to America."

Two opposite thoughts collided in my mind. The danger: It was rumored that border patrols killed escapees caught crossing into Poland on the spot; and the thought of living in the "Goldene Medina" (golden land) suffused me with happiness.

"Not a word to anyone." my mother cautioned. "We must do all our planning in secret."

My mother got her older brother, Itske, to accompany us on what would be a three-day horse and wagon trip from Bobruysk to Minsk, where he would help us find a smuggler to get us across into Poland. That was the general plan, but the preparations had to be well thought-out. Informers swarmed in Sitskeveh and Bobruysk among some of the most unexpected neighbors, from children to the elderly.

Minsk was about 100 miles west of Bobruysk, the focal point for those who, for whatever reason, were desperately anxious to escape into Poland and beyond. Smugglers eager to earn quick money, using various forest pathways under cover of night, in horse and wagon, were managing to take hundreds of their human cargo into Poland. But it was rumored that hundreds more were either killed or arrested, depending on the whims of the Bolshevik border guards. Only brave smugglers and their brave passengers were among those who attempted to cross the dangerous forest border. My mother and aunt had the reasons and the courage to brave the dangers.

To avoid detection by neighbors, we devised a plan where we would start from Krevoya, a small village 15 miles from Bobruysk, where we had relatives, and there arrange to have a large wagon with two hitched horses waiting for us. My mother and I would leave for Krevoya a few days earlier, before her sister and children would leave Sitskeveh to join us.

Early in the morning on a cold autumn day, with my uncle Itshe at the reins, we began our journey to America. For an hour we rumbled on a narrow dirt road until we reached the main, hard-packed wide road to Minsk. We ate the bread and baked chicken our relatives in Krevoya had prepared for us, and by evening Itshe turned off the road into a clump of trees, where he fed the two horses, climbed into the wagon, and we all went to sleep. It was a cold night, and we snuggled and nudged each other for mutual warmth.

At the break of day, Itshe fed the horses, hitched them to the wagon, and we were off again. The sun came out to help thaw out the chill in our bones. The scenery began to change. Instead of passing through thick forest as on the first day, small villages occasionally interspersed the landscape. At the opening clearing of one of these hamlets, the sight and stench of several human corpses stirred gasps of fright from the elders and tense curiosity from the children. I kept gazing at the bodies until they were out of sight. Several miles further there was a lone corpse on the other side of the road.

Fright turned to alarm as we made our way to what lay ahead. We didn't have long to wait. We heard a sound and a dim sight of an automobile in the distance, and as the monster of a truck roared past us, our horses reared and turned on their side, turning the wagon with them, and spilling all of us into the road.

My uncle, who was a big, strong man, scrambled up, and within a few minutes straightened the horses and wagon. He then looked at his cargo of passengers sprawled on the ground.

"Anyone hurt?" When no one complained he said, "Climb back into the wagon while I calm the horses."

By evening, shaken by the sight of corpses, the capsizing of the wagon, and tensed by the continuing cold, we again pulled into a grove of trees on the side of the road and tried to rest in sleep. It didn't come soon. Most of us were conjecturing about what the next day would bring.

The next morning began a cold, cloudy day. I was wide awake, geared for any new incident that might come along. Nothing happened, but by evening our food was almost gone and all of us were physically exhausted.

"We're famished and too cold and tired to spend another night in the wagon," my mother complained while her brother was looking for a place to park for the night. "Shouldn't we try to look for a home nearby, and offer good pay for food and lodging for the night?" My aunt and the children echoed eager agreement. A half-hour later as the shadows of trees were beginning to form across the road, the welcoming dim lights in homes shone through an opening in the forest. Itshe stopped at the first farmhouse. A burly peasant came out to question the strange intrusion.

"Can we stop for the night? We're – " Itshe asked.

"I'm not interested," he cut in sharply, and shut the door.

Itshe drove to the next farmhouse. A woman met him, with a man close behind her. Itshe repeated his request about spending the night, but this time she let him finish his request.

"Come on in and warm up," she greeted us, but without the man's acquiescence.

"You don't know who they are," the man cautioned, but not too strenuously.

"Can't you see where they're going," she brushed him off.

"You talk too much," he scolded.

"That's because I know more than you what's going on." She turned to us, "Climb out of the cold wagon and come into our warm house."

We paid her in advance and she prepared a wonderful meal, spread blankets on the floor, and we enjoyed a warm night's sleep. In the morning, refreshed by a hearty breakfast, we dawdled a bit too long with the gracious hostess, knowing we had only a half-day's travel to Minsk. As we were loading our baggage into the wagon, three soldiers on horseback rode up, Vladimir of Sitskeveh among them. My mother was first to react. "What brings you here, Vladimir?" she asked in a half-frightened, half-friendly voice.

"What are you doing here?" he flung back sarcastically. "You don't have to tell me, I know. And you're all under arrest."

"What did we do? We're only going to visit our relatives in Minsk," she lied. "What's wrong with that?"

"What's wrong is that you're planning to escape into Poland. That's what's wrong." He turned to his two companions, "Get all of them into the house, search them for hidden money. And then, turning to my mother, "I'm taking you to the Minsk commandant, and he'll decide what to do with you."

"Vladimir," my mother beseeched him in a begging voice, "remember when you had a high fever and I brought leeches from Bobruysk to suck the fever out of your body to get you well. Doesn't that count?"

"Nothing counts more today than what's good for communism. I have no more time for you." He turned to the soldiers. "You know what to do."

When I heard Vladimir say that they were going to search everyone, my mind quickly turned to the rubles my mother had sewn into my undershirt. What do I do? My 11-year-old mind was mature enough to seek an answer. When we were herded into the house and told to undress and remove our shoes preparatory to being searched, I rushed up to Vladimir, and with a grimaced face, palpitating voice and hands on my stomach, burst out, "I've got to go!" and without waiting for an answer, I rushed to the outhouse about 50 yards away. When I got in, I ripped the patch from my underwear and stuck the money in a crack, put some bits and pieces of dirt over it, and with a victorious feeling, walked back into the house. After searching everyone, including the children, the only money found was in my aunt's clothes.

"The children can remain here, or come to Minsk. We're only interested in the adults."

My cousins chose to go with their mother; I chose to remain with the friendly couple. My victory about the money was short-lived, as I waved, with tears running down my cheeks, to my mother and the others as the wagon turned into the main road to Minsk.

The first thing I did was to go back to the outhouse and retrieve the money. Buffeted and educated by a bombardment of dangerous trials, I was developing practical insights beyond my age.

After two weeks of living in suspension between not knowing what to do next, and my hosts' visible impatience with my stay, I revived enough courage to offer them 20 rubles to take me to Minsk and help me find out what happened to my mother and my relatives. After some discussion between them, they agreed.

I was filled with childish wonder at my first sight of Minsk, compared to Bobruysk. The buildings were bigger, the cobble-stoned streets were wider, and more people were hurrying in the streets. Horses and wagons were parked next to the buildings. The couple found the office of the commandant where, after checking with several officials, they located a young lady who gave us the information that all were released and had left except Sifra Stanek who was sick with pneumonia, and was waiting for her son before going back to Bobruysk.

When I saw my mother's emaciated face, I rushed and buried my head on her neck in a torrent of tears.

"Oy my sonnele" she sobbed, "at least we're together again."

Our hosts were told that there was a train leaving for Bobruysk that night. "Will you have the strength to go?" I asked.

"Yes, yes," she sobbed.

Our hosts helped my mother into the wagon and drove us to the rail depot. They helped her into an empty boxcar (it was a freight train) and I climbed in after her. The inside was dark and cold. Our clothes provided little warmth against the penetrating raw air. We huddled in each other's arms, I giving her the warmth of my body, and she giving me what was left of hers. The loud rattling of the wheels below mingled with my mother's moaning as we clung to each other in our waning strength without food or water. That torturous night train ride has remained the most vivid, searing incident in my memory.

When the train stopped and I saw streaks of light through the cracks around the door, I felt a new burst of energy surging through me. I opened the door and recognized that it was the

Bobruysk depot. I bounded out of the boxcar and hailed a man to help me get my mother down from the elevated opening. I then found someone to go to Yankev and have him come with his horse and wagon to take my mother home. Yankev came, helped her into the wagon and to the first warm meal and bed since the ordeal of trying to cross into Poland.

Chapter 4

My Mother's Bravery

Only those with pluck and fearlessness attempted to escape Russia in the aftermath of the Revolution. And my mother was one of them.

After a month of convalescence, my mother got her robust vitality back, and with it her unrelenting desire to leave Russia for America. Despite the warning by the jailers in Minsk that if my mother and her sister were caught preparing to escape, punishment would be death or Siberia, she hatched a plan to try again. Her sister was not as sanguine, but my mother got her to agree.

The plan, as I heard it, would have Fruma and her children leave Sitskeveh at daybreak and meet my mother and me at the rail station to board the train for Minsk. This would cut short any preparatory detection. After the details had been worked out, we met at the station and, with dozens of other passengers, squirmed into a huge boxcar, similar to the empty one that took us from Minsk to Bobruysk.

Within several hours, a stench permeated the stuffy air, but despite the discomfort, a few hearty passengers began singing old popular ditties, and others cut them off by singing the Communist Internationale. I was surprised at the friendly, humorous banter that ensued because I was conditioned to fear informers of the "whites" or "reds." When the train reached Minsk, and the doors were flung open, utterances of joyous, fresh air relief, passed through the crowd.

But our relief was short lived. A greater problem than foul air confronted us. What do we do next? We had no plan other than to separate our families and walk slowly, with our bags, away from the railroad station. After 10 minutes of aimlessly walking to nowhere, a young lady, who had watched us from afar, approached my mother and said bluntly, "I know what you're looking for."

"How do you know?" my mother answered guardedly, fearing she might be an informer.

"I know the signs. I have a horse and wagon nearby. Get the other family members to come with you and I'll take you to my father who will get you across to Poland. Do you have the money?"

"Why should we trust you?" my mother said half-heartedly.

"You have no choice, and I suggest you make up your mind quickly because the longer you dally, the more chance you'll attract an informer."

My mother made a quick decision. "We have the money and we're going with you." She walked over to her sister, told her what she had decided, and still separately we followed the young stranger the short distance to her horse and wagon.

A half-hour later she stopped at a house with a big yard and a huge barn at the end of it. She drove into the barn, where a large wagon, several horses, and piles of hay scarcely left room for our horse and wagon. We left our bags in the wagon and walked into a large room similar to our home in Bobruysk, a brick oven in the center with cloth partitions as bedrooms on the perimeter. A short, husky man with a swarthy face and piercing dark eyes greeted us with the same directness the young woman did.

"I know why you're here, and you know why you're here. My daughter explained it to you. Crossing into Poland is a dangerous undertaking. You cut down some of the danger with me because I've bribed a few border patrol and I know of safer paths through the forest than most. But the danger is still there. You've chosen to face it, and so have I with every crossing."

"Have you ever been caught?" my mother asked.

"If I had, I wouldn't be here!" he said unsmilingly.

"When do we leave?" my mother pursued.

"The first dark night."

In the evening, two days later, he briskly announced, "We're leaving tonight." He led us into the barn, told us to spread our baggage on the bottom of the big wagon, and then showed us how to cover our sacks of baggage with our bodies in a way that our heads faced the perimeter of the wagon. We saw the common sense of this arrangement when he covered us with a huge load of hay, our nostrils close to air. After he attended to several details so that our load looked like a typical wagon of hay, he hitched on two horses and we were off.

I peeked through a tiny opening through the hay and watched the lights and wondered what kind of people lived in those homes. After a half hour of city views, the lights were blotted out as we were completely enveloped in forest darkness. I had no idea whether we were following a narrow road or pathless forest. I was frightened when I heard the faint neighing of horses, and on one occasion our horses responded. When that happened, the smuggler stopped our progress, and from what I heard, dismounted from the wagon to calm the horses. As we moved along hour after hour without incident, my initial fears relaxed. Perhaps this smuggler knew how to avoid dangers. Lulled by this optimism, I even closed my eyes for a few minutes to snatch some sleep. It was longer than a few minutes, because I was awakened by the stirrings of my neighbors and streaks of light streaming through the hay. After about an hour the horses stopped and I heard our driver announce, "You're in Poland now."

My heart beat with happy excitement as I scrambled from under the hay, the first of our group to step on Polish soil. An open area dotted with several farmhouses greeted my eyes, a village about half the size of Sitskeveh. When the others climbed out from beneath the hay, the smuggler led us into the house where he had stopped, and where he apparently had been before, and said,

"My friends here will give you food and lodging for a few days. My work is done. I'm going back to Minsk after I get a few hours of sleep, and after it turns dark. You're now in this couple's care."

As young as I was, my antenna was already able to perceive that we were not in friendly care. He was a big burly man with a sullen face, and his wife was a diminutive woman with shifty, sly eyes that kept ogling our bags. After the smuggler left, the little woman, with a bright kerosene lamp in hand, didn't ask but ordered that we bring all our bags and open them for her perusal.

"Your rubles are no good here," she said in Russian, "so we'll have to take some of your things instead." And without waiting for the sisters' reaction, she began to rummage through one of the larger duffel bags. She picked up and looked gleefully at my mother's black silk scarf, one of her prized possessions, and put it aside. After she collected a dozen sundry things – towels, dresses, pillow cases – she stripped my mother's watch from her neck and her sister's necklace and rings. When they tried to withhold their heirlooms, the man sidled up and said, "You better comply."

The loss of precious things mixed with our gratitude for food and a warm house. But the dominant question that seared our immediate thinking was how and where do we go from here? We didn't have my uncle to help us, and the couple was growing surlier by the hour.

On the third day of our stay, a horse and wagon drove up and a young man came to the door. He said something in Polish to our hosts, then walked inside the house and began a long explanation to us in Yiddish.

"I know why you're here, and I'm here to help you. Let me explain. People in America make donations to an organization known as HIAS, Hebrew Immigration Aid Society. It hires people like me to help refugees like you to get to America. I make a sweep every several days here to look for stranded families. I'm going to take you to Horodock, a slettel [village] about 10 miles from here, where you'll live for several months until I get proper papers for you to travel to Warsaw. I'll tell you more on the way to Horodock."

We all listened with rapt attention. When he stopped, my mother burst out, "You're not just a young man, you're an angel from heaven. God has sent you to us."

After a pleasant ride during which we peppered him with questions and he answered them politely, we came upon quite a large village and he stopped in front of a large white house. "Here's where you'll spend all your days until you're ready to legally take the train to Warsaw."

We were very fortunate. We had surmounted the dangerous life-and-death part of our journey, and we were settled in with a friendly Jewish family among many native Jewish families who also housed refugees. While working for our traveling papers, the refugee and native Jews formed a togetherness to celebrate birthdays, holidays and other happy social events. A brand new emotion overwhelmed me at one of these. A dark-haired, dark-eyed girl my age stirred an urge I had never experienced before. When I asked who she was, a Horodock young man told me she was the daughter of a wealthy Jewish man who was rumored to be involved in smuggling. "A real beauty, eh?" he quipped.

At one of the social gatherings I saw her dancing with someone, and when my mother noticed me watching her, she said, "Go ahead, son, ask her to dance." Well, I didn't know how to dance, and besides, I didn't dare talk to her; I only fantasized what she might say. Before I fell asleep that night the new, exciting emotion kept me awake for hours, and for weeks afterward, because I didn't know how or dare to tell her how I felt.

My new phase of handling pleasure was shattered by a tragic event that shook the Jews of Horodock. In the dead of night robbers got into the smuggler's home, took the goods he was rumored to have accumulated from his business, and killed everyone in his family. I was devastated. My mother grieved, but not with the intensity I did. She understood, and let me cry without trying to console me. "What good is it to be rich?" she philosophized.

Our host couple had three children, and one girl was close to my age. Though she was attractive, she did not evoke my young male hormones, especially when after a slight altercation, she hit me with a spoon across my nose, which left a deviated septum over my right nostril that is still there today.

After five months of leisurely living, our angel from HIAS showed up with the good news that he had the passports, with which to travel to Warsaw. I had mixed feelings. I had become used to not having to face new dangers. My mother and aunt Fruma, however, were delighted. When we got on a train at a small railroad station about 20 miles from Horodock, and a gendarme looked at our papers and waived us on, I sighed with relief.

After a day of uneventful travel, we got off at the huge Warsaw railroad depot where another HIAS man met and drove us to a huge apartment complex. It was similar, as I would one day recall, to the movie "Milo 18" where the Nazis met opposition from a handful of Jewish fighters during World War II. Our HIAS host led us through labyrinthine hallways into the fifth floor of this residential armada that overlooked a huge square open area around which rose eight walls checkered with small windows.

After we settled and began to get used to the strange sardine-like environment, I probed some of its strange features. I went into the basement and walked some of its labyrinthine passages, but not too far for fear of not finding my way back. I mingled with the sales people in the open area market surrounded by four walls where they hawked their wares and food; residents came down daily to do their shopping. The buyers were native Poles, Jews, and a sprinkling of refugees like us. The bargaining that went on was new to me. I understood it when it was in Yiddish, but not when the haggling was in Polish.

We never got outside of the apartment complex for fear that we might get into some sort of trouble, but I liked to mingle with the people in the marketplace, where I picked up some Polish. "Yak she mash." (how are you) and the response, "Dobshe" (good), "Kabusta" (cabbage) and a few swear words, too obscene to translate.

I was beginning to enjoy the camaraderie of strange but peaceful people, when my pleasant complacency was suddenly jarred. Our HIAS lifeline guide to America hurried into our apartment and shattered our normalcy with, "Pack your things and be ready to leave by train to Volomin tomorrow morning. We've learned that the Polish authorities intend to make a sweep of this building, arrest refugees who've escaped in Poland and deport them back to Russia. Be ready when I call for you." And without stopping to answer our questions, he hurried out.

We packed in a hurry, and after a sleepless night, we were picked up early in the morning and driven to the railroad station where we boarded the train for Volomin. An hour later, and about 25 miles away from Warsaw, we alighted in a quaint village, and were driven by a waiting HIAS man to a house a short distance away. When my aunt, her children, and my mother and I were settled, the young man gave us instructions how to conduct ourselves in our new "home." "Most of the people here are not friendly to Jews, so keep to yourselves and don't irritate any of them. You may have to live here for months. A man by the name of Jake Ulevich of Milwaukee, in America, is working on your visas. As soon as we receive them, we'll deliver them to you with advice on what you should do next, because from then on you'll be strictly on your own."

Life in Volomin was not life threatening, but miserable. The people eagerly accepted our Zlotes (Polish money) for the goods in their stores, but treated us with disdain and ridicule when we tried to speak in halting Polish. The children had a more difficult time. When I left the house, a few days after we arrived, to explore some of the adjoining streets, two boys my age ran up and started beating me. As a result, we languished in the house with nothing to do because we could see the urchins waiting for us to come out.

After being cooped up for months, I decided to brave a walk to a nearby lake that I remembered was a short distance from Volomin. I was rewarded for taking a chance by the sight of a beautiful crystal-clear blue body of water surrounded by luxuriant trees. The sylvan scene was marred by a man with a rifle who was shooting at a duck in the water.

I sat down on a stump of a tree and watched the life-and-death battle between the hunter and his prey. As soon as the duck surfaced he would raise his gun and aim, but by the time he pulled the trigger, the bird would dive under the surface and appear again in a few minutes some distance away. This went on for another half-hour until the hunter gave up and walked away. This poignant scene left an indelible mark on my memory, and it may have initiated my strong feelings for the underdog; just as my being smitten by the dark eyed 12-year-old girl in Horodock initiated my feeling for romance. That's how seeds sprout.

After almost a half year of living amidst the hostility of our older neighbors and constant fear from the younger ones, the lifeline to America opened. Our HIAS savior came in one day and with a big smile announced, "Your visas have arrived!" Those spine-tingling words swept me into a sense of happiness I never experienced before. I didn't know the meaning of ecstasy, but I certainly must have felt it. So did the others.

Chapter 5

The Torturous Watery Crossing to America

What lay ahead of us were hardships rather than dangers. We took the train to Warsaw and from Warsaw to Danzig. There we were ordered to be deloused under hot showers in a huge building before getting into the ship to cross the North Sea to England. The next day we were driven to Danzig's seaport, where I was overwhelmed by my first sight of our huge ship and awed by the vast stretch of water that ended in the sky instead of an opposite shore like the wide Bergezina River in Bobruysk.

I was thrilled by the spectacular scene, but that exuberance soon changed when we were led, with about 300 other immigrants, into the bottom hollow of the ship. The first thing that hit our nostrils was a strong stench, and our eyes scanned a huge dungeon-like room strewn with leftover debris across a dirty wooden floor. Each family unit picked a small area and settled down in it for the duration of the voyage. Each family was given blankets for beds, and after about half an hour, when the several hundred families had stretched themselves out on their bedding, we heard three horn blasts followed by a reverberating noise as the motors revved up for the voyage. Soon we felt the movement of the ship, heard another three whistle blasts, and we were off.

During the first hour the small waves were pleasant, but soon the ship began to heave, and within another hour there was a heaving of food as passengers joined in a cacophony of moaning and vomiting. My mother was one of them. The stink from the outhouse-type lavatory, the smell of disgorged food, the roaring of the motors and the retching sound of vomiting, made life for my mother agonizingly unbearable. She was the most sensitive of our group.

I was wobbly, but mobile. What affected me the most was the nauseating smell of cooked food. But that wasn't enough to stop me from wanting to climb the stairs to the upper decks, even though we were told they were off limits for the immigrants. I wanted to sneak up when it was daytime so I could see the waves. Stealthily, I climbed four flights of stairs and opened the door to broad daylight. I quickly walked over to a rail, and what I saw left me breathless with fear and amazement.

I saw mountains of water rising toward the ship, lifting it up and then plunging it in a huge hole of water, where the ship righted itself upward and charged ahead. I wasn't scared when a wave lifted it up, but when it fell, my heart fell with it. I was mesmerized by the battle between the "tiny" ship and the mountainous waves, and amazed that the ship won with every heave and plunge. I was so entranced by the spectacle that I wasn't aware how the fresh air fueled my body with new alert energy. After several hours, I reluctantly left the bit of heaven for the hell below.

After three torturous days for my mother, we docked at the port of Liverpool, England. My mother had to be carried off the ship on a stretcher. During the next five days, while waiting to board our ship for America, she regained some of her strength, and eagerly asked people how the next crossing would compare with the last one. "Worse," they told her because the Atlantic crossing would take 17 days. My mother and I, with heightened curiosity on my part, and apprehension on hers, readied our wills for the last episode of our long-lasting escape to America.

The lower hull of our larger ship had the similar stench, dirt, and roar of motors as the smaller one, but instead of 300 immigrants it held twice as many. The first few days it was relatively calm and only a few were heard with the usual symptoms of seasickness; but then we hit a storm, and pandemonium broke loose. Hundreds were retching, crying and vomiting on the floor and accidentally on each other. My mother was among the first to succumb to the storm, and a day later I too became immobile. I was so sick that I had to forgo my several hours of watching the waves from the upper decks.

On the fifth day, what was bearable during the three days on the smaller ship, became unbearable here. The prospect of 12 more days of this added mental and physical misery. "Oy my son-nele," my mother said in a weak whisper, "if I knew I would feel so miserable, I wouldn't have left Russia."

There were times when, with my last bits of energy, I had to find a doctor from the upper deck to see my mother because I was afraid she was dying. All he did was give her a pill and left. The air was permeated with the stench that came from both ends of the passengers. During the last few days, my unbearable nausea made me unrealistic enough to agree with my mother's desperate wish that we had remained in Russia rather than suffer this tor-ture.

When my mother and many others were carried off the ship on stretchers at Newfoundland, Canada, where we docked, we had several days of rest before taking the train to New York and Ellis Island. My mother's resiliency was remarkable. Spurred on by wanting to look her best before meeting her husband, she managed to get her eyes shining with happy expectancy.

We saw my father waiting for us after we passed through Ellis Island. My mother rushed into his arms. I didn't know how to react. After my parents unclasped, I beheld a sturdy, five foot little man with a mustache – a complete stranger. I didn't know what to do, and neither did he. We were both inexperienced in handling this awkward situation. I walked up to him, but couldn't say anything with the word "father." Neither did he find anything to say with the word "son." Silently we hugged each other, as my mother looked on smiling with delight. After a short embrace, he walked back to my mother and they had a lot to reminisce about.

The chilly greeting with my father thawed a bit on the train from New York to Milwaukee, but through the years it never reached the warm ambience I enjoyed with my mother. The eight years of absence had left a gap that neither of us could fill.

With our arrival in Milwaukee, my Russian life ended and the American adventures began. Starting as an illiterate 12-year-old in a strange land, my trials were different than the Russian tribulations. My physically harrowing experiences prepared me to handle stoically the mental challenges that faced me in America.

Part

2

My Life in America

Chapter 6

My First
Schooling Adventures

T he first day I walked out of my home on 7th and Lloyd Streets, I was met with the stark reality of not belonging in America. The people on the street talked in a babble I didn't understand, and the signs on the corners were words with no meaning. And to compound my frustration, I faced an awkward dilemma. My mother's older sister, Michla, who left for America before the World War, lived with her husband and four children in the flat below us. Her children were completely Americanized. They neither spoke nor understood Yiddish. This was my language barrier's first and foremost frustration.

Aunt Michla took charge of Americanizing me and Aunt Fruma's four children. She enrolled us in a special school for "greenhorns." My first day at school was like walking into the biblical Tower of Babel. People were talking in many languages, and young and old had different dress and looks – Jews, Germans, Czechs, Poles, Russians, Italians, Norwegians – raw recruits who later melded into the American melting pot.

As my eyes roamed across the hall, the first and most impressive thing I noticed was how peacefully all these different people were getting along. A woman teacher with several aides soon came in and asked the some 200 pupils to sit down at the tables, and the way she did it was for her helpers to translate it in several languages. What followed in the next days, week and months were eight hours of daily drilling in learning the meaning, pronunciation, and reading of hundreds of English words, then phrases, sentences, paragraphs, pages, and then reading easy-to-understand books.

After a year of "greenhorn" schooling, some graduated at the third-grade level, some at the eighth-grade, and I graduated at sixth-grade level. At our graduation ceremonies, I was chosen to recite The Pledge of Allegiance, and after practicing it dozens of times at home, I delivered it without a hitch, and walked off the dais with a pride that surpassed everything I had ever done before.

I faced a multitude of new challenges when I left comfort and familiarity of the greenhorn class for the mainstream of American education. Miss Wolsky, my sixth grade teacher, greeted me with a special friendly accord because of my foreign status, but it didn't allay my fear of having to compete and cope with my young American peers. I was three years older than the average sixth grader, and that bothered me. How would I relate to mere innocent children after what I had gone through? And I was ashamed of my foreign accent.

When, after a few weeks, I heard Mariea recite "The Wreck of the Hesperus," and compared it with my rendition of The Pledge of Allegiance, I trembled at what I was up against. But to buoy my spirits, I told myself that the challenges facing me were not going to be as great as those coming to America. But then I always had my mother at my side; I reflected that now I had to face my new challenges alone. It's time I told myself.

These ruminations boosted my self confidence, and I plowed into my sixth grade work with the intensity of those who study for their doctorate degrees. Arithmetic was most difficult; geography was totally new and difficult; and English was the easiest because it interested me the most. I noticed that most of the students rarely took books home. I rarely missed taking an armful home to study. As hard as I worked, my report cards never showed a mark above B minus, while two boys who befriended me and never took a book home, got nothing but As. They more than befriended me, they helped Americanize me. The clever 11-year-olds devised a deal that involved my paying them a nickel for every time I mispronounced a word. I had the most problems with Vs and Ws; and so they would catch me saying "wery vel" instead of "very well."

My nickels bought them many ice cream sodas, and brought me closer to sounding like an American. I owe a debt of gratitude to Joe Gorsman, who became a prominent orthopedic surgeon, and Herman Hurwitz, who became a lawyer and was chosen number one saxophonist of Wisconsin. They shepherded me through my difficult grade-school days and, in many ways, through high school.

High school challenged me with a new problem: teenagers who aroused my libido. Mature girls in the full flower of their youth filled my eyes with desire for their companionship. But those who attracted me the most paid no attention to me, and those who didn't appeal to me didn't care for me either. I was confident that I could converse more interestingly than many, but being only five-feet-five, with a foreign accent, I was no match for robust football players, track men and six-foot-tall Americans. I tried to meet that competition by going out for football, but when the coach looked at my 120-pound body, he said, "Young man, they'd crush you. Football is not for you."

So I admired the beautiful students from afar and kept my sexual urges bottled up. It gave me more time to dig into my scholarly work, where the competition was fierce. I studied more than most of my classmates. Gradually my interests and capabilities shifted toward English. *The Last of the Mohicans, The Call of the Wild* and books about Daniel Boone entranced me to the extent that I wrote book reports for myself to get the full flavor and excitement of what I read. Authors became my heroes. And because I spent no time on girls and sports, and more time on my studies, I graduated from high school in 3 1/2 years.

Life in college was a mature undertaking – the change from boys and girls to men and women. I was amazed how much more mature and intelligent the students at the University of Wisconsin were compared to men and women their age in Russia – like two different breeds of people. And the professors appeared to me like masters of wisdom, a level above mere human beings. To mingle with people like these was worth all the travail I endured coming to America.

However, my life at the university was no lark. All my father could afford was $15 a month for meals and I shared a tiny room with another student in a dilapidated house facing an alley entrance. And my sparse clothes matched my father's frugality. But my mind never rested on these shortcomings; it soared on economics, social issues, and on *The Magic Mountain*, a book by Thomas Mann. The more I delved into secular subjects, the less I gave time to my religion. But to be versed in the rudimentary knowledge of the two religions, I read the Old and New Testaments. It changed my orthodox idea of a personal God, to a God who was the main character in the Bible story. It confused rather than clarified my idea about God.

The Ten Commandments were my mother's God, and I was suckled and weaned on their strength, but my Commandments were now more diluted. While I was a sophomore, I was tested; how much was my orthodox religion ebbing away? While I was on a second walking date (I couldn't afford more) with a student from one of my classes, we stopped to rest at one of the benches off the path that circled around Lake Mendota. It was a beautiful April twilight evening, and after a bit of conversation, I decided to steal an innocent kiss. I didn't have anything more on my mind than that.

But not so with her, because she turned to me and blurted out in an excited voice, "How would you like to end our walk in a hotel room tonight?" and with a coquettish smile added, "and it'll be my treat." My first reaction was shock, followed quickly by an aroused libido, and then a few seconds of wavering. I made my decision and phrased it awkwardly. "I don't think so, I'm sorry."

This short, inadequate answer was followed by two awkward silences, and as I walked Betsy to her dormitory, I felt good that I didn't give my virginity to a brazen woman in an ordinary unromantic way.

Joe Waxer and Joe Goodman were my closest friends in college. They were go-getting, good guys who helped me get out of my tendency to spend more time with my books than with students. They were gregarious and happy-go-lucky; I liked their company. And they had knack for business.

The early 1930s were Depression times. Students were organizing scalping schemes to sell tickets at football games at a profit. My two friends were in the thick of it. "George," they told me, "you're not cut out to be a businessman, that's why we didn't invite you in."

"I'm not so sure I'd be interested," I said. "What if you're caught and suspended from school?"

"Not if you know your way around," they smiled smugly.

All that interested me in the midst of all this scalping mania was to sell my roommate's and my tickets at the regular price of $3 each. When I got to the football gate, I asked a gentleman if he wanted to buy my tickets.

"You're under arrest" and he put his arm on my shoulders.

"Wait a minute," I objected. "I'm a student and only trying to sell mine and my roommate's tickets at the regular price because we need the money more than our desire to see the game. What's wrong with that?"

"How do I know you're not a scalper?" he said in a somewhat believing, friendly voice.

"Do I look like one?" I smiled.

"Yeah, I guess not. Why don't you celebrate my leniency by getting your roommate to enjoy the game with you."

"Thank you. I'll take your advice and treat ourselves for finding an understanding guy."

When I told my two friends who were deeply involved in scalping, they laughed at my amateurishness and Joe Goodman, in an authoritative tone said, "George, I told you, you're not cut out to be a businessman." It was only a boyish opinion, but subliminally it had the effect of nudging me toward a writing career. But at the same time I didn't want to let go of their friendship for fear of becoming a loner. My two friends helped me solve that problem.

After one of their successful ticket-scalping football games, they invited me and a girl I was dating occasionally, for dinner followed by a three-date canoe ride on Lake Mendota. As we were returning our canoes to the dock, and mine was about 30 feet from the landing, my girlfriend stood up in preparation to step ashore. She tipped and fell into the lake. Without thinking, I jumped in after her. We both stood up in three feet of water. Joe Goodman and Joe Waxer didn't stop laughing as my date and I walked dejectedly to the dock. Fortunately, there was no one around except the dock boy.

Drenched to my bones, I turned to my friends and begged them not to give this story to the *Cardinal*, the student newspaper. "You can depend on us," Joe Goodman promised. I was relieved, but not for long. The next day, I read this headline on the front page of the *Cardinal*: "Our Student Hero Jumps into 3 Feet of Water to Save His Date from Drowning." I was devastated. For a month I was greeted with shouts from far and near with "my hero." I cringed, I smiled, and I finally waved nonchalantly in a humorous exchange to soften the hurt of their mocking banter. It was the price I paid for being "one of the boys."

But my two friends paid a bigger price to be with the "big boys". They were caught scalping and were expelled for a year from the university. It changed their careers. It stopped their intention of becoming lawyers.

Chapter 7

Carving a Career

The exuberance of walking from the podium with my diploma faded after a few days, and was replaced with the stark reality of "What do I do with my education to earn a living?" I now reflected that had I enrolled in a technical school where I could have learned a craft instead of educating my mind with literature, sociology, and philosophy, I would be more prepared to earn a living. Yet I was glad I had seeded my mind with the big and important issues of the world. I would be barren without them. Also, I liked writing, and without a college education, I would have no background for it.

I consoled myself with the idea that I could get a job as a newspaper reporter or in an advertising agency. The two daily newspapers gave me a "no" with the explanation that newspapermen with many years' experience were walking the streets without jobs. A dozen advertising agencies gave me the same "no" with the same explanation. But one, a Mr. Rieselbach, took the time to advise me to test my writing skill by submitting a feature article to the *Milwaukee Journal* Green Sheet, which published articles by freelance writers.

This suggestion fit in with my love for writing, and I didn't waste any time looking for an interesting story. A Russian immigrant whom I knew when we attended the "greenhorn" school together, told me that John Barrymore of Russia had escaped to America, and that he was now living in Milwaukee; but more importantly, the former actor knew Rasputin, the famous Russian monk who had mesmerized and controlled the life of the Czar's wife.

I interviewed the famous Barrymore, and after a week's work I submitted the story to the *Milwaukee Journal*. The editor accepted it, and gave me a byline to the 1,000 word feature. I was ecstatic. Never mind that I received only five dollars for it; the thrill was that I was a published writer. A month later I sold them an article on "How to Get Your Man," a lighthearted feature, and got 10 dollars for it.

A couple of months later I sold the Green Sheet on a series of articles describing the characteristics of the various nationalities living in Milwaukee. I interviewed representatives of 18 different nationalities, ran the series once a week, and was paid $100 for 18 weeks of work. I liked the experience and the publicity, but not the pay.

I was impressed at seeing myself in print. That was what prompted me to take the big gamble of taking a year off to write a novel. I had already titled it in my mind – *Bobruysk*, with the subtitle *In the Aftermath of the Russian Revolution*. I announced my decision to my parents, and they said it would be wonderful to have a famous son.

To use a trite expression, it was a labor of love. I bounded out of bed, and after a hurried breakfast, I wrote all day long without getting tired because my creative juices were flowing abundantly. An interesting phrase, a unique insight, an unusual plot angle, thrilled me to the point where at the end of the day I felt the night got in the way of my joyous hours. My health was at its best, getting along with my parents was never better, and my friends praised my keen sense of humor. It was a glorious year. After I had proofread the manuscript for the fifth time and had it typed by a professional typist, the first one I showed it to was my friend Rieselbach.

"Please take whatever spare time you have and read my year's work. I know it's an imposition, but it is because I value your opinion so much that I took this bold step."

"I'll be glad to read it," he replied in his usual friendly manner. "Come back in about a week."

Ten days later, full of optimistic anticipation, I walked into his office. After exchanging a few friendly niceties, he pulled the ground from under me with his first sentence.

"George, I'm going to be brutally frank. Your novel doesn't have the slightest chance of being published," followed by reasons so convincing that they flattened all the inspirational bubbles I had in defense of my joyous labor. He saw the sadness in my eyes, and to buoy my spirit he suggested that I seek another opinion from the editor who published my feature articles in the *Milwaukee Journal*. I grabbed on to the scintilla of hope that perhaps an editor might be a better judge of literature than an advertising man, but I wasn't walking on air anymore, only on hard reality.

The editor was a kindly man who must have seen my struggles through his eyes when he tried to break into a writing career, because he promptly agreed to read my manuscript. A week later he called me, and when I sat down across from him at his desk, I had worked up my imagination to the point that he had my writing future in his hands. He got directly to the point.

"Young man, you talk more convincingly than you write. My advice to you is that you'd have a brighter future in business than in a writing career. Your novel has some interesting stuff, but not nearly good enough to interest a publisher. I suggest that you view the year spent on your novel as a magnificent failure leading to a successful career in business. Talking benefits to people can be as rewarding as, and certainly more profitable than, writing on blank sheets of paper."

I left the editor's office more dejected about my novel than elated that I talk more convincingly than I write. My sadness was based on the stark reality of failure, with little uplift on the ephemeral "maybe" that I might be successful in business. The editor's suggestion elicited the memory of my college friend Joe Goodman's remark, "George, you're just not cut out for business." And what further pushed the business idea into a far-fetched possibility was that I was not prepared for it because none of my college courses dealt with business.

Gone were the happy days when I jumped out of bed eager to work on my novel. Instead I lazily lay in bed and had to force myself to get up and face another empty day. Worries of remaining an unemployed nobody began stealing into my psyche. I envied people who had their minds focused on work, unlike my mind which roamed dejectedly from one unreal nowhere to another, and coming back to endure my real nowhere. I envied my father, who had a shoe repair shop to go to every morning. I even began to wonder whether a literature major who graduated the same time I did, didn't have a better answer to my empty hours with his plan to sell watermelons during the summer and hole up in a one-room garret to write poetry during the winter. For months I suffered the agony of filling my empty days with thinking too much and doing nothing to extricate myself from my mental quagmire.

One afternoon, while I was walking in a secluded Lake Park ravine, thinking about my plight, a bombshell of an idea stopped me. Why not start a magazine catering to the fledgling liquor industry, now that the Volstead Act was repealed? As I walked home, my pace was a lot faster than when I left home, and my mind quickened because the idea combined my love for writing and a chance that the editor's opinion might have some validity. My creative juices began flowing again, more in the direction of the magazine's literary content than how to make it profitable. I had saved $300 from my freelance writing and selling shoes on Saturdays, enough I thought to print 1,000 copies of the first issue of the magazine which I titled *Beverage Guide*. After I discussed my plans with Mr. Johnson of the printing firm, Dozie and

Johnson, he said, "I'll do it for you for $300, which is below our cost, to help you get started, but be prepared for higher costs once you get going."

I immediately set out to write the copy for the magazine. I was satisfied with the subjects I chose: "The History of Alcohol," "Why Alcohol is Embraced by all Societies," "How Different Grains are Creatively Used to Produce Alcohol," "The Difference between Refined and Rowdy Drinking." Halfway through my writing I realized that to pay for printing and make a profit, I had to get someone to sell advertising. I hired a Mr. Monzingo, who had a gift of gab, a quality which I thought made a good salesman. We agreed to divide 50-50 the revenue he produced from selling the advertising. The first issue of *Beverage Guide* came out with $200 of paid advertising and Monzingo kept all of it.

"I need the money very badly," he said, "but I have promises of about $600 or more for the next issue. I'll credit you with your $100 then." I had no choice but to believe him – reluctantly. The second issue came out with $460 of paid advertising, which we divided equally, but without the $100 credit. Monzingo was full of promises for the third printing, but one morning there was a knock on my door, and before I could say "come in," two men walked in and without a word sat down on the two chairs across from my desk. They kept their wide-brimmed hats on as they looked around the room. I broke the ominous silence.

"Well gentlemen, what brings you here?"

The older man answered in a gruff, whiskey voice. "We're coming into Wisconsin with a pulp weekly newspaper called *Tavern News*. We're starting off with 3,000 and we'll get up to 10,000 as new taverns open up throughout the state. We checked you out. You're doing it all wrong with your slick monthly magazine with stuff that doesn't interest tavern-keepers. We're backed by the Wisconsin Tavern-Keepers Association. What they want is news about their business, not fancy history about alcohol. We've checked you out. You're a nice young man, and we'd be willing to pay you $10 a month to be one of our editors. We advise you to fold up and come with us. We'll be back in a week for your answer." Without waiting for what I had to say, they got up and left.

I didn't take a week to decide. I had enough common sense, if not business sense to see that what they told me was good advice rather than a threat, even though their rough manners suggested it. And to soften the blow, I wasn't as fulfilled writing about the beverage business as I was writing feature articles, not to mention my *Bobruysk* novel. And to clinch my decision, bowing out of *Beverage Guide* was to be rid of the awkwardness I felt when at tavern meetings I had to exchange drinks, which got me dizzy at best and sick at worst. When I added it all up. I soothed my disappointment with the reasoning that perhaps those two men saved me from a business I would not be happy in – even if I were successful.

A week later, as they promised, the two men came in and without any preliminary talk asked, "What's your decision?" I was just as direct. "I'm taking your advice and closing down Beverage Guide."

"You've made a wise decision, young man. What about working for us as editor?"

"I'm sorry, no." I copied their abruptness. But they surprised me when before leaving they shook my hand and the older man said, "You made a good decision."

I was cast adrift again. The previous ennui came back with double despondency. I had failed as a writer and now as a businessman. I revisited my pre-*Beverage Guide* thoughts about my future. With my writing and business ventures proven failures, what was there more for me to try? Was I doomed to remain a nothing? Day after day, week after week, despondent thoughts fed on each other and I could tell it was beginning to worry my parents. They said nothing, but I saw that my worry was their worry.

I could tell that my mind was sliding into sadness and I began looking for a resource to liven it, a digression, some mind steadying interest. But what?

After some introspection I realized that I was thinking too much about girls and not enough about other things. I had a strong desire for the companionship of women but I had ignored it because of my intense desire for a career. I was poor but there were many poor women available who had a strong desire for the companionship of men. I threw myself into dating for two reasons: I liked their company and dating was a therapeutic antidote for my despondency. The lighthearted evening banter was good for the ladies, and doubly good for me. It cleared my mind for several hours of the worries and anxieties that plagued me.

But there was a hitch. Of all the girls I dated who kept me afloat on cheerful thoughts, one in particular, Adeline, gained more than my ordinary attention. She was attractive, gracious, intelligent. I was beginning to feel the pangs of love. But there was a problem. She lived in a duplex on Lake Drive, a residential mark of wealth. That bothered me. Would I be comfortable with her rich parents? But what I admired about her was that she never hinted that she was special because of it. She hobnobbed with the west-side poor boys and girls without ever calling attention to where she lived.

I began to date her often, and then exclusively. But the joyous moments with Adeline created a problem. I began to flirt with the idea of proposing marriage, but there were two obstacles. The first was the possibility that she might turn me down because I had no future career, and that would sink what little self-esteem I had left. The second was that if she said yes, my fears for the future would double.

A new thought crept into my uncertain mind. Was it fair, keeping Adeline on a string to soothe my turmoil and not care about plans she might want for her future? It was the first time I began thinking beyond my own welfare. I began seeing Adeline less and less and then cut it off completely.

Breaking off with Adeline left a hollow in my mind that was now filled with self-deprecating thoughts about failing in writing, in business, and now in romance. I dramatized my plight by thinking that while millions of people had their cups running over, others half-full, mine was completely empty. Perhaps, I thought, I was aiming too high, that I'd be better off by lowering my expectations and trying something as mundane as selling real estate on commission to fill my empty hours.

I figured that it would not be difficult to get a company to hire me because it would have nothing to lose. I chose Sandler-Schneider, a small two-man company. They were middle-aged gentlemen who operated on a small scale, Sandler concentrated on mortgages, Schneider on selling homes. I passed the real estate examination to be certified as a real estate salesman, but with an apathy that sharply contrasted with the enthusiasms when I began writing my novel, and when I initiated the *Beverage Guide* venture. Another way of describing my attitude was that I sadly began to drown my sorrow in selling real estate.

Chapter 8

I Discover the Sales Power
of Benefiting People

A calm came over me when I joined Sandler-Schneider. Gone was the turbulence that filled the vacuum of my mind when I woke up to an empty day with nothing to do except think about my sorry plight.

My lowered expectations found a comfortable home in the waltz-time pace of Sandler-Schneider. David Sandler spoke slowly and leisurely with his mortgage clients. David Schneider preferred to deal with home buyers in his office after they were shown the premises by owners. He rarely drove buyers to sellers' homes. But because both Davids were well known in the community for their integrity, they managed to eke out meager means for their families. When inquiries came in for listings, David Schneider was happy to turn them over to me. Our arrangement was to split 50-50 the commission on the sale of houses. The standard commission was five percent of the sale price.

During the first month I obtained several listings. I showed about a dozen prospects through our listed properties, with nothing close to a sale. Both partners cautioned me not to be discouraged. I wasn't downhearted because I began to value the peace from being involved with people. Each one had a different story, a different dream about the biggest purchase of their lives.

I was undergoing an important change. Instead of thinking how to benefit myself, as I had during the past few years, I became more and more interested in how to benefit others with the knowledge I had to help them. The benefit idea grew

into an ideal. Unlike David Schneider, who seldom drove buyers to sellers' homes, I not only showed them through our listings in which they showed an interest, but drove them to see
other brokers' listings to enlarge their exposure to find homes,
even if it meant less commission for me. During the drives I
explained why a 30-year amortization is more desirable than
a 20-year because the monthly payments are lower, how a
half point in lower interest rate saves thousands of dollars in a
30-year mortgage, where to get and how to finance a home
improvement loan, and other practical real estate advice.
Because I practiced my selling with genuine benefit fervor, I
could tell by their responses that they appreciated it. I was
amazed how much I began to enjoy their camaraderie, their
friendship, their dreams.

My first sale was a $10,000 duplex. I earned the phenom-
enal sum of $250. It spurred me on to concentrate on my ben-
efit idea, and within six months I earned $2,000. I discovered
a virtue on the firing line of action which I failed to find by
reading the Old and New Testaments. Interacting with ordinary people like myself was teaching me that serving people
benefits the server as well as the served. It planted a seed in my
mind that sprouted in later years.

By April, 1937, I had $5,000 in the bank, and I confi-
dently began searching for a mate. Adeline was gone, engaged
to be married. I looked into my little black notebook where I
had written down the names of girls through the years who
attracted my attention. One of them was Mildred Davidoff, a
shy 16-year-old girl I met at a party when I was 20. I remembered that she had lipsticked and mascaraed her face to look
older because most of the girls and boys at the party were four
to five years older. Because she was pretty and looked scared,
I befriended her to ease her immaturity. She was too young for
me to follow up my interest, so I lost track of her. Six years

later, an act of serendipity brought us together again.

On a sunny Saturday May afternoon while I was walking on Bradford Beach, I noticed a girl in a blue bathing suit who reminded me of Mildred Davidoff. Could it be? I ruminated that she might actually be the 16-year-old I met at a party six years ago. Spurred on by the confidence of success I now enjoyed, I walked up to her, and after noticing how filled out she was in the most interesting places, I asked, "Could it be that you're Mildred Davidoff?"

"Could it be that you're George Bockl who was nice to me when I needed it?" She showed none of the timidity I remembered six years ago. She introduced me to the companion sitting next to her. "This is my sister Anita." We reminisced about the time we first met, and about the years that intervened.

At one point during the conversation I said, "Are you still as innocent as when we first met?"

She smiled and parried, "It depends what you mean by innocent."

That was an appropriate time to spring what was on my mind, "Would you have dinner with me so we can discuss it at greater length?"

"Yes, that would be a lot of fun."

And that started a torrid courtship that was mutually conducted on a high moral plane. Her high standards helped keep mine there also. In addition to being pretty, she was intelligent and sparked a keen sense of humor. And physically she had all the attributes that allure men. She was the second youngest of three sisters and two brothers who all lived in a large apartment because they were too poor for the older children to live separately. Her father was a clothes designer who moved his family to cities where he could obtain work. Mildred worked in a low-paying job as a bookkeeper for a company that placed peanut vending machines in stores and restaurants in southern

Wisconsin. She knew poverty as I did, but it didn't cast a shadow on her joyous personality.

Four months after meeting her on Bradford Beach, I geared myself up to ask the question I had been hesitant to ask Adeline. With confidence spurring me on, I chose a fine restaurant, and after an hour of fun repartee, I changed to a serious demeanor and heard myself saying, "Millie, I love you, I want you to be my wife." It sounded stiff but serious enough to startle her.

She composed herself quickly and in an equally serious voice said, "George, I'm sorry, I promised to be engaged to an attorney in Chicago."

My cup of high expectations drained to the last drop as she explained that her boss had her meet his brother-in-law in Chicago, who proposed marriage within a few weeks. Delicately, but frankly, she said, "Not knowing your intentions, and while you waited, he acted and I accepted. George, I'm very, very sorry, and frankly, a bit confused."

I listened with rapt attention and then made a quick decision on how to handle the unexpected turndown, the loss of all the dreams I wove around our future happiness.

"Millie, I'm devastated. That says it all. But because I love you I wish you a life of future joy and happiness."

We didn't say much as I drove her home, but at the door I gave her a long, lingering kiss and left.

I turned my full attention to my work. I asked my bosses to let me put more zing in the advertising and they readily agreed. Our responses doubled. "No wonder," David Schneider said, "I heard you're a writer." I began to sell a property every other week, mostly as a result of being invited to prospects' homes for meals and family celebrations. Elderly immigrant Poles, Italians, Swedes, and others were intrigued when I told them that I was an immigrant too. And because I was able to discuss some of their characteristics from remembering the articles I had written about the various nationalities in the *Milwaukee Journal*, they welcomed me as one of them. Referrals poured in and I was kept busy 12 hours a day, seven days a week. I suggested that we hire another salesman, and they did.

Sandler-Schneider became a beehive of activity. The harder I worked, the stronger I felt physically, and more fulfilled mentally. The therapy of keeping busy helped allay my despondency over losing Millie. Whenever the loss stabbed my memory, I cut it off with the insight that dwelling on it fatigued my mind with might-have-beens instead of soothing it with pleasant memories.

During the Thanksgiving and Christmas holidays, a new feeling suffused my mind – a sense of gratitude for my good fortune. My agonizing days changed to joyous ones. My act of desperation when I joined Sandler-Schneider turned into one of celebration. I was experiencing for the first time the happiness of success. In my exuberance, a happy thought popped into my mind. Why not send a card to Millie, wishing her happiness in this and all future holidays? I sent it off with many other holiday greeting cards to my social and business friends. Two days later as I rummaged through my mail, my heart leapt with joy when I saw a card from Millie. It read: "Thank you for your thoughtful holiday wishes. I sincerely wish you the same. Also, I'm happy to tell you that I broke off my engagement. With all my pleasant memories I am sincerely yours. Millie."

A flood of ecstatic feelings swept over me. I read the phrase, "I broke off my engagement," over and over again. It sent a thrill every time. I was enveloped in a cloud of euphoria. Good fortune was pouring in on me. When I snapped out of my reverie, I noted that she was true to her non-aggressive nature. She didn't ask me to call her. But it didn't stop me from calling her within minutes after I got my emotions organized. I phoned her at work. "I read your note. Will you see me tonight?"

"I'll be delighted," She purred, and that was enough for me to conclude that she reopened the door to our former relationship.

When I called for her, and fortunately she was alone, we flew into each other's arms and without a word our spontaneous embrace sealed the vows of engagement and marriage. What followed was a resumption of our courtship and after seven months of blossoming love, we were married on June 26, 1938.

Chapter 9

I Launch into Entrepreneurialism

W ith the confidence of a superb love life and burgeoning business success, I began to hear entrepreneurial rumblings coursing through my mind. My main sticking point was: Should I give up sure success for an uncertain future? I posed my indecisiveness to my wife. Without a moment's hesitation, she said, "Go to it, honey, I have the utmost confidence in you." With her enthusiastic support and my chomping at the entrepreneurial bit, I took the bold step of cutting my umbilical cord from the safe haven of Sandler-Schneider to facing the uncertain realities of self employment. There was no hitch in the parting. I thanked them for giving me a successful start, and they thanked me for livening up their partnership.

I rented a small office, hired a part-time secretary, and placed a series of sizzling ads in the *Milwaukee Journal* citing the reasons why homeowners should choose George Bockl Enterprises to sell their properties. The response was beyond my expectations. And the sales that followed dissipated all my fears about starting my own company. I joined the Milwaukee Board of Realtors, part of the national association that set the agenda for the ethical conduct and promotion of real estate commerce. I was proud to be part of an important profession.

Spurred on by my conviction that my ideal of benefiting people had catapulted me into where I was today, I began seeking practical ways to benefit people who in turn would enhance my business. I noted that I sold some homes in a matter of days, others in weeks. I placed an ad in bold print: *WE CAN SELL YOUR PROPERTY IN 30 DAYS. PROOF: SOLD 1818 KINNICKINNIC*

IN 17 DAYS, SOLD 2518 MINERAL STREET IN 14 DAYS, SOLD 2108 CENTER STREET IN 23 DAYS.

A flood of calls followed, but so did a call from the ethics committee of the Milwaukee Board of Realtors.

"Your ad is not a violation of any law," its spokesman said, "but it's a departure from our custom of listing properties for sale for six months. Your ad rocks our tradition that has served us well for many years."

"We're in the business of selling properties," I responded respectfully, "if an idea doesn't violate any law and sells properties faster, why not try it if it benefits both realtors and those we serve? Why not call it progress? I'm proud to be a member of the Board of Realtors, and you can count on me to uphold its high ethical standards."

As we were walking out of the meeting room, Ray Hiller, one of the ethical committee members, put an arm around my shoulders and said, "Young man, I don't think you'll have anything to worry about from the Board of Realtors."

"We can sell your property in 30 days" proved to be a bonanza beyond my expectations. I needed help to handle the calls. I decided not to advertise for salesmen but to hand pick them.

While I was in the kitchen reading the newspaper, I heard a vacuum cleaner salesman tell my wife in the living room the benefits of his particular brand of cleaner, I was impressed. I went in the living room after my wife bought his vacuum cleaner and asked, "How would you like to sell bigger things than vacuum cleaners?"

"Like what?"

"Like homes."

He smiled. We chatted. A month later Gus Wand became a real estate salesman.

I attended an amateur play, and the lead actor was exceptionally good. After the applause at the end of the play, I walked over to him and asked, "What do you do for a living?"

"I'm not ashamed, but proud, to tell you that I'm in charge of a garbage collection unit on the south side of the city."

"How would you like to sell real estate?"

"Who, me? Are you kidding?"

"No, I'm serious."

We talked for a few moments while people were waiting to congratulate him. Three months later Ted Marks began working for George Bockl Enterprises.

Under various situations, I recruited part-time school teacher Ralph Schwartz, former farmer John Hazelfield, former naval officer Milton Begel, attorney Joe Zilber, former prison guard Spike Kallas, accountant Jack Tarnow, unemployed violinist Jim Hatzie, Horace Rosen, housewife Julia Tennenbaum, and, ironically, my unemployed college friend Joe Goodman who prognosticated that I was not cut out for business. Eventually my two unemployed brothers-in-law, Milton and Ray, became part of my sales force.

I bought a building on the corner of 16th and Vliet Streets. By 1947, I employed 45 full- and part-time sales people divided in two offices – one on the north side, managed by Paul Spector, an attorney, and the other on the south side, at 13th and Lincoln Avenue, managed by Jack Tarnow, the accountant. All were well versed in the sales power of benefiting people. However, to keep 45 highly motivated men and women busy, I had to find new ways to create more merchandise for them to sell.

I initiated three untried sales ideas that mushroomed our sales activity to the point of keeping two attorneys busy closing deals at the rate of one a day. Idea number one consisted of buying group buildings on one lot and subdividing, or as it later came to be known as "condominiumizing" – that is, selling the buildings to different owners. I originally got the idea when six dilapidated cottages on one lot on 7th and Meinecke Streets were offered to me for $6,000. They had a history of being sold and resold as low-end investment properties. I bought them and sold each one for $1,500. Within a year, the former blight became an oasis of rejuvenation. The new hands-on owners changed the wooden foundations to cement blocks, repaired and painted the wood siding, upgraded the plumbing, and replaced wood-burning stoves with furnaces.

The six new owners were happy with their accomplishments, the neighbors were happy with getting rid of six eyesores; but it did not please the real estate editor, Bill Manly, of the *Milwaukee Journal*.

"Bockl has created legal pandemonium on 7th and Meinecke," he wrote in a stinging feature article on the rudimentary condominium project. "Who owns the walkways between the cottages? Who is responsible for the common sewer lines, water lines, electric lines leading into the cottages? Bockl's created a legal mess and future litigation."

But contrary to the real estate editor's predictions, the six owners had no problems, and a few resold their homes at a profit with no legal ramifications.

I bought dozens of group properties and subdivided them, thus providing hundreds of sales commissions for my employees.

The idea of splitting ownership of group properties to many individual ownerships flushed out a flurry of benefits: blight was eliminated in many parts of the city; the social good of many new homeowners in contrast to ownership by less concerned speculators; hundreds of thousands of dollars of work for craftsmen; and profit for my company. It was so well accepted as a boon for the city that Bill Manly invited me to be the guest speaker for the Midwest Conference of Real Estate Editors to explain the "condominium" idea.

Idea number two was financially complicated, racially sensitive, and socially rewarding. The challenge was delicate and difficult: how to construct a plan to sell homes to African Americans who had little cash for a down payment and not substantial enough jobs to collateralize a home loan. I devised a plan that solved both problems. Here is a concrete example how it worked, how it moved 1,000 African-American families from their ghetto to nearby white neighborhoods. I would buy a home in a white neighborhood about a mile or two from what was considered the ghetto for $10,000 from an owner who wanted to move farther out. I would personally sign a mortgage for $8,000 with a savings and loan company and sell the home to an African American for $13,000 with a $500 cash down payment, with the buyer assuming the $8,000 first mortgage and signing a second mortgage of $4,500 with the same rate of interest as the first. The 30-year amortization payments on the first and second mortgages were usually not much more than what the buyer was paying in rent. In order to get my $1,500 cash back I had in the property I would sell the $4,500 second mortgage for $3,000 in cash, thus getting my $1,500 back out of the transaction and $1,500 profit.

At the risk of being immodest I have to say that, the benefits that flowed out of this unusual home financing were phenomenal. A thousand renters enriched the city by becoming proud homeowners. The savings and loan companies earned millions of dollars in interest from the loans they made to me, which were subsequently assumed by the home buyers. The homeowners who lived close to the ghetto area were able to sell their homes for cash and buy other homes elsewhere.

Many white owners who remained in their homes where African Americans moved in, became socially and racially integrated. The investors who bought the second mortgages at a good discount received huge returns for their risks because the properties went up in value, which secured their investments. My salesmen benefited from the hundreds of sales to African Americans, as well as from the hundreds of sales to those who wanted to move farther out. I profited from the number two idea because I increased my sales volume.

Those who benefited the most from the idea were the 1,000 African-American families who moved out of the ghetto to a new neighborhood into their own homes. During the years that followed, with minor exceptions, I did not lose any money in collateralizing several millions of dollars in loans for African Americans, those who risked buying the second mortgages were paid, with very few losses, and the African Americans who bought the properties sold them at a profit and moved farther out.

The finance idea benefited everyone who participated in it. It was a big win for enlightened capitalism.

The third idea involved the weaving in of a whiff of spirituality into my work, with the result that I learned how the secular and spiritual reinforce each other. The appreciation I received from African-American families suffused me with a different kind of feeling than the reward of business success. One was fulfillment, the other excitement. When I became aware of the difference, I wanted to experience the same sense of fulfillment in dealing with my salesmen as I did with the African Americans.

The small shoots sprouted into lavish proposals to the salesmen. I would split the profits with the salesman who had purchased a property for Bockl Enterprise; he would receive an additional commission when it was sold. This arrangement quadrupled the earnings of my top salesmen like Joe Zilber, Gus Wand, Joe Mandel and others, who earned from $40,000 to $60,000 a year, a huge sum in the early 1950s. What was equally rewarding was that all my salesmen became my close friends. We became a large family of workers. And whatever minor disputes arose between salesmen or between salesmen and me, were heard and settled by three salesmen judges.

Collateralizing loans for African Americans, and doing the same for whites who couldn't qualify for loans, and not losing any money in the process, bolstered my benefit ideal and rewarded me with genuine fulfillment. And splitting the profits in the buying segment of our operation – without the salesmen taking any risks in collateralizing loans and thus earning much more than mere commissions – rewarded me with their appreciation, friendship, and camaraderie. All this, which I dubbed "enlightened capitalism," sent a new idea coursing through my mind: Why couldn't this enlightenment be extended to other facets of our life? Synchronicity – how one thought attracts another parallel thought – did it for me, as it has done for millions of others.

Chapter 10

Moral Rearmament

I n the early 1950s, while my wife, I and our three children were vacationing at the Grand Hotel on picturesque Mackinac Island, Michigan, I noticed a huge sign, Moral Rearmament, on one of the old mansions facing Lake Michigan. Out of curiosity, I looked into its open door. I was greeted by a young man with an English accent who courteously asked me if I would like to meet some of his friends. When I agreed, he led me into a large room where he introduced me to a teacher from Burma, a student from Japan, a Zulu chief from Africa, a labor leader from Ohio, and some 20 other men and women from different countries, races, and cultures.

After the gracious introductions I could hardly contain my wanting to know more about what I was seeing. I turned to the Englishman and asked, "Would you please tell me the purpose for these different kinds of people congregating here? I'm puzzled and I'd like to know more."

The Englishman smiled. He was obviously ready for such questions. "We're here to attend a World Conference on Moral Rearmament starting tomorrow morning and you're invited."

"But can you give me a short explanation of Moral Rearmament?"

"I'm going to give it to you in a nutshell, but please come tomorrow to hear it in full. We're on a quest for a universal spirituality that will unite the spiritual longings of people from all different races, cultures, and religions."

"What will do it, and where do we find it?"

"What will do it is changing our human nature, and where we

can do it is during a daily meditation while we're seeking God's guidance for life."

"Does it work?"

"Come to the conference and find out."

The next morning I walked into a huge hall where about a thousand people, in their native dress, gave me the feeling that it was a blown-up picture of what I had seen in the mansion on the lake. One of the leaders of the conference, with a Scottish brogue, greeted the audience with divine language, but I liked it best when he said, "We are here not to engage in platitudes and become spiritual dilettantes. We are here to witness the practical proof that seeking God's guidance during a daily hour of meditation can actually elevate our human nature from where we are to where we see more, comprehend more, and enjoy more. You will hear amazing stories of how and why people changed their shoddy views to sublime values."

From about a dozen amazing stories of people who shared their experiences from the podium, the following were the most fascinating. I paraphrase these stories in the first person to get the full intimate flavor of their experiences.

An American writer. "I'm a writer. I was sent here a year ago to write a feature story about MRA, (Moral Rearmament), with a slant to show that it was a throwback to the Victorian Age. I holed up at the Grand Hotel with a couple of bottles of Scotch and began interviewing some of the leading MRA people. They responded to my questions with gracious candor. After two days of abrasive questions and friendly answers, they asked me to try an hour of meditation. For kicks, I did. Nothing happened. Please try it once more, they said. This time a brand new thought crept into my mind. I compared myself to them. I was a phony; they were genuine. They stood for something; I stood for nothing. I stayed a few more days. During the ensuing meditations I discovered a lot of things I didn't like about myself. Was I getting closer to God with my honesty? Whoever or whatever God is, seeking guidance was making me a better person. I remained on the island for several weeks, learning more about how seeking God's guidance was changing my human nature. I didn't write the story. I still write, but with meditative guidance, with a changed human nature."

A Swedish go-go girl. "I'm a modern Mary Magdalene who changed with the help of the same God power that changed Mary 20 centuries ago. My parents were divorced in Sweden and I came to America with no greater goal than to earn my keep go-go dancing in nightclubs. One day an apartment neighbor asked me to have lunch with her at a gathering in Los Angeles. After lunch a young man my age told a group of about 20 young men and women how he was freed from promiscuity and shoddy living by seeking God's guidance during a daily quiet time. He was so different from the young men I knew, so honest, so believable. He told us where he hung around, which reminded me of where I hung around, and how changing his human nature liberated him from the tacky life he was living. I was moved by his story. He struck at the sadness underneath the cheap life I was leading. He challenged me, and the others, to see what we'd find when we sought God's guidance during an hour of daily meditation. I tried it again and again until I found the joy of changing my human nature. That's why I'm here – to share what I've discovered."

A Kenyan terrorist. "I worked as a teller in a British bank during the day and burned white settlers' homes at night. This was my way of fighting for Kenyan independence. I was caught and jailed. One day a British officer walked into the prison compound and addressed a group of prisoners. I was amazed to hear him say, 'I want to apologize for our British superiority, but neither do I condone breaking the law. You're here because you want things your way and we want things our way. There is another way. Is there anyone among you who would like to find out what it is?"

"I was the only one who volunteered. There was a chorus of angry murmuring, and someone shouted, 'It's a trick!' Another yelled, 'Traitor!' I walked out with the British officer amidst the jeering of my cellmates.

"I spent a month with my British friend on Mackinac Island where I was transformed by the MRA wisdom into a new man. My friend and I went back to Kenya and together spoke before hundreds of white and black audiences, offering spiritual reasoning for a peaceful transition to independence. Newspapers in Kenya applauded our new ideas, and many editorial writers went as far as claiming that our conciliatory efforts saved thousands of white and black lives before Kenya won its independence. Moral Rearmament has the spiritual wisdom to change people like me, who in turn change others to use peaceful means to change dangerous situations as we've done in Kenya. MRA points to the Power that changes people if we take the time to listen to its wisdom."

Italian Communist. "I've written marching songs for Togliatte, Italy's Communist leader, urging faceless millions to gain more freedoms from capitalist dictatorial oppressions. But I was a dictator at home. My wife and daughter feared me. I gave them no rights to make decisions. One day a man challenged me with an idea that he claimed was more revolutionary than communism. What is it? I asked. 'Moral Rearmament,' he said. 'Oh some religious idea,' I quipped, 'not interested.' He persisted, and I finally agreed to go to Mackinac Island.

"What impressed me most about the men and women I met was their complete honesty, in contrast to having to be on guard in dealing with my comrades. When I tried meditation, I was confronted with many of my dishonesties. For the first time I was disturbed by them. After a week of daily quiet times I was moved to cleanse myself of all lies by calling my MRA friends in a room and having them witness my apologies to the people to whom I'd been lying in absentia, with a promise that when I go back to Italy I would apologize to each one personally.

I know it sounds unbelievable, but to my amazement and to the amazement of the people when I got back to Italy, it really happened. A mystic power changed me when I listened. People call it God. It's the same thing. Communism is one of many man-conceived revolutions, but the final revolution is believing in the mystic power people call God, the same mystic Power that changed my human nature."

I spent several days on the island. I got the reaction from those who met MRA for the first time, talked to those who've been in it for several years, and to a few leaders of the MRA idea. One evening I took my family to see "The Forgotten Factor," a play that depicted a struggle between the self-serving reasoning of a labor union and the self-serving reasoning of management, and how the spiritual reasoning of MRA solved it into a win-win for both. I managed to have lunch with the writer, the speaker who impressed me the most.

"MRA," he explained, "is a daily cleansing of the struggles, self-serving calculations, anxieties, and fears that pollute the mind. Seeking God's guidance is a humble admission that we don't know it all, that we need help to cope with the fog and debris that circulates in our mind. If we let go during quiet time, we invite the flow of cosmic energy – God – to renew our body and illume our mind with new ideas that lead to inspired living. If it has done it for a hard cookie like me, it can do it for anyone."

When I ended my vacation and went back to business, I was too busy to think about MRA. But the urge to try it was murmuring in my mind. The first few trials were failures. Business agenda crowded my quiet times. But I persisted, and soon new thoughts began to mingle with the mundane and I perked up to take notice. The thoughts were not only new, they stirred me to re-evaluate those I lived by. Often there was a clash, and I sought guidance as to which was closer to the truth. I became so interested in the challenge that I started a journal, and after each quiet time I would write a terse résumé of what went on in my mind. I began to look forward to each meditation with a sense of anticipation for new ideas to challenge those mired in old thinking. I found daily meditative guidance to be a rewarding and enriching experience, a practice I've kept up to this day.

Chapter 11

MRA in Action

Here are a few of the hundreds of thoughts from my journal which challenged my mind during the many years of quiet times. For the sake of brevity, I offer them in headline form.

Anyone Can Be a Healer

Free Will – a Tyrant or Angel?

Why Practicing Enlightened Capitalism Is Greater than any Art

Why We Need the Transcendent Right Brain and Practical Left Brain to Reinforce Each Other

Why Trusting People Is a Good Gamble

Why We Should Be Wary of Charisma

Why Are We Normalizing Cultural Abnormalities?

What's Beyond Being Smart, Intelligent and Wise?

Why Those Who Put Themselves on Display Do not Brightly Shine

Why It's Wiser to Observe More and Opinionate Less

Seeking Daily Guidance Is Exploring the Invisible for Visible Human Progress

How the Dark Side of Winning Is Poisoning our Culture

The Difference between Spiritual Self-Discipline and Religious-Imposed Discipline

I have expanded each of these and many other ideas into 200- to 300-word essays, which the following three examples will illustrate.

CHANGING HUMAN NATURE MORE
IMPORTANT THAN CHANGING INSTITUTIONS

We've overemphasized the importance of changing institutions and underestimated the significance of changing human nature. One deals with surface, the other with depth. The best institutions can be corrupted by bad people. You can't make a good omelet out of bad eggs.

Though laws and political systems modify human nature to some extent, they do not effect a profound change. Did the Russian people change when they bloodily cleansed themselves of Czarism and converted to Communism? Weren't Stalin and his hordes crueler than the Czar?

When Republicans take over from Democrats, or vice versa, do the leaders and their followers change? Does the Far Right, which clings to its conservative institutions, and the Far Left, which hews to its liberal institutions, have anything to do with elevating human nature? Hardly!

Changing people is the forgotten factor of our civilization. We forget, at our peril, that 2,000 years ago a wise man gave his life to show that it is more crucial to spiritualize humanity than to cling to self-righteous religious institutions. His wisdom profoundly changed more lives than all the changes made by all the institutions during the past 20 centuries.

LISTENING TO GOD,
A MORE RELIABLE GUIDE THAN PEER ADVICE

When we seek guidance from God's silence, we receive responses that are more elevating, more reliable than the advice we get from our peers. Although we may enjoy their companionship and friendship, their counsel does not have the same clarity of insight that comes from meditative quiet time.

This comparison is not ephemeral imagination. It's common sense. Daily quiet time, transcendental reflection, and reading spiritual literature are the most reliable guides for organizing the bits and pieces of experience into an orderly whole, which is a prerequisite for a fulfilling life.

Does God speak to us during meditation? Definitely, yes! From where else can we get our insights to advance evolution? It guides, heals, and renews us whether we're aware of it or not. That's a more intimate and more profound form of communication than the sound of a human voice. And when we're inspired by a noble idea, or beauty in nature, we're actually communicating with God, the ultimate intelligence of the Universe. Thus, there's a constant dialogue between God and man, and the more we become cognizant of it, the more guiding insights will flow our way. Therefore, it's wise to keep our end of the line open so we can receive God's messages from the other end of the line.

THE DIFFERENCE BETWEEN
FEMININITY AND FEMINISM

The feminist clamor for equal status with men is good and bad. It's good for procuring equal rights; it's bad when women try to act like men.

The macho mindset of husbands who run their families like owners, coaches, and quarterbacks is an anachronism that should be changed, especially the tyrannies of husbands who abuse their wives and children. All good men should rally behind feminist demands to eliminate this long-standing injustice.

However, an increasing number of feminists are clamoring for equal status in unnatural ways. When a woman sheds the honey of her feminine allure to ape man's aggressive speech and mannerisms, she loses a precious part of her mystique. She violates the law of natural opposites.

The ideal relationship is for the wife to play the role of equal partner (never subservient), and for the husband the role of protector (never domineering). The children, then seeing the mutual fusing of parental roles, will emulate their elders and thus strengthen family ties.

The feminists ought to use their skills to obtain equal rights everywhere, but never rob men of the joy that makes them strive with accelerating heartbeat for the delight of a woman's natural enchantment.

I've written hundreds of short essays like these for my journal, and had about 60 of them published in the Op-Ed page of the *Milwaukee Journal* during the ensuing many years. Of the various comments I received, the Op-Ed piece on "The Difference Between Femininity and Feminism" elicited the most interesting commendations from the most unusual sources – a rabbi and a priest.

I could tell that my human nature was changing as a result of attending the school of wisdom, as I called my seeking God's guidance half hour to an hour a day. I saw more, comprehended more, and enjoyed more. I approached my secular activity with more equanimity. I had a clearer view of why and what was going on in the world, and what was motivating people I dealt with daily.

It dawned on me during one quiet time session that these private communications with God were bettering me, and indirectly bettering others from my win-win benefit ideal, but in addition to getting fulfillment, I was also getting an accelerated monetary return.

How about doing something for people, I asked myself, that has no monetary return – only fulfillment? It didn't take long for synchronicity to answer my question.

I had read in the *Milwaukee Journal* that there were about 100 large, poor families living in rat-infested basements, and that the Milwaukee Welfare Department was paying high rent for them because landlords refused to rent the better flats to hard-using, large family tenants. About the same time I learned that the Federal Government had offered a new program known as Title Five that financed homes for poor large families at one hundred percent, up to $35,000, with the provision that payments on the mortgage be amortized over 30 years at 4 percent interest. The sound reasoning behind this plan was that the payments on the mortgage by the Welfare Department would not be much more than the rent it was paying for the welfare recipients in unsanitary basements. And there was another beneficial provision for the poor, large families. They would become the owners of the new homes, and social workers would be assigned to help the families manage the intricacies of home ownership.

I bought 21 vacant debris laden lots from the city at $100 apiece, 10 of them located on the north side in the Afro-American area, and 11 lots on the south side in the Latino area. I hired Dennis Sobenski, a recent college graduate with a major in all facets of real estate, to take charge of building 21 new homes, each not to exceed $35,000. I called Larry Katz, Federal Housing Administration Director in charge of implementing Title Five, to help Dennis with the immense paperwork involved in processing the construction of the homes. I agreed to pay Dennis $18,000 a year for the two years that it might take to get the 21 families into their new homes. My contribution to the project was limited to what I paid Dennis and my time supervising him. All the rest was paid for by the government through Title Five.

This private-public partnership went through without a hitch except for one poignant incident. During the early stages of the venture I was asked by an executive of a television station to explain the benefits of Title Five. Father James Groppi, a white priest who led a group of Black Panthers to protest anything that they found wrong in the community, was in the audience with his Panthers. After I explained the details of the program and urged others to get involved, the moderator asked

Father Groppi what he thought of it.

"I don't trust these sleazy real estate guys," he said. "They always have something up their sleeves."

The moderator turned to me. "What do you have to say to that?"

The Father got my dander up and I flung back, "Since when, Father Groppi, do you have a moral monopoly in our community?"

Before I was about to make a few more comments, a Black Panther rushed up to the podium and was about to punch me when my African-American companion, sitting next to me, who was part of the program, put his hand up and in a no-nonsense voice said, "Cool it Johnny, maybe he's got something good for us."

"Okay," Johnny said as he was walking back, "but no one talks back to Father Groppi." The meeting ended amicably.

I visited the large families in their new homes. They were slow in articulating their appreciation in words, but I could tell it was deep and sincere. In one home, a four-year-old took me on a tour. I was thinking, as I watched the happy faces, how a small amount of my money lifted 21 families out of dilapidated basements into new homes of their own. Of course, this could not have happened without a strong partner: a caring government.

My seeking guidance to elevate my human nature did not interfere with my pursuing business success. On the contrary, it clarified my real estate thinking. They worked in tandem, each enriching the other. While I was enjoying my double interest, a new universal spiritual idea lifted me beyond my religion, beyond MRA, and into a new cosmic view of our relationship to God, man, and the Universe.

Chapter 12

I Meet Theosophy

A New Thinking Spiritual View of the World

One day a professor of philosophy at the University of Wisconsin-Milwaukee, with whom I was slightly acquainted, stopped by my office and put a magazine on my desk and said, "George, I know of your interest in MRA, and I know how it has changed you, but this "Theosophist" magazine will take you from where you are to a new realm of ideas that will drastically change your view of God, your relationship to man and your understanding of your role in the Universe. It's not a religion, cult or some guru's spirituality. It's the latest spiritual research of dozens of sages from over 50 countries. They have built their new universal spiritual thinking on the ancient religious wisdom and on scientific evolutionary knowledge that is available today, but was not available in the past."

When he left I picked up the "Theosophist" magazine and I read "The Three Objects of Theosophy":

1. To form a nucleus of the universal brotherhood of humanity, without distinction of race, creed, sex, caste, or color.

2. To encourage the study of comparative religion, philosophy, and science.

3. To investigate unexplained laws of nature and the powers latent in man.

The Three Objects were accompanied by an illuminating short essay on "Freedom of Thought" followed by an explanation of Theosophy's universal spiritual wisdom, of which the following is an excerpt:

Theosophy is the body of truths that form the basis of all religions, and which cannot be claimed as the exclusive possession of any. It puts death in its rightful place, as a recurring incident in an endless life, opening the gateway to a fuller and more radiant existence. It restores to the world the Science of Spirit, teaching man to know the Spirit as himself and the mind and body as his servants. It illuminates the scriptures and doctrines of religions by unveiling their hidden meanings and thus justifying them at the bar of intelligence, as they are ever justified in the eyes of intuition.

This was heavy stuff and, had I not gotten my feet wet in MRA, I probably would not have waded into it. Fortunately, or I should say, synchronistically, both happened at the right time.

I was swept into a new world of wonder and challenge when I read the spiritual literature of the theosophical pioneers; H. P. Blavatsky from Russia, Annie Besant from England, Sri Ram from India, James Perkins from America, and others from other countries. What drew me to the people I met who studied Theosophy was that they did not try to promote, proselytize, or claim some supernatural knowledge, they politely asked me to explore the new ideas that will shape the world of tomorrow. They claim, but without any charismatic bombast, that their universal new spiritual thinking is as crucially important for our time as Moses', Jesus' or Mohammad's revolutionary ideas were for their times.

After reading and discussing the theosophical thinking with many spiritual pioneers, and adding my own interpretations and evaluations during my daily meditative quiet times, I was moved to paraphrase a few of the leading ideas as clearly as it is within my capacity to do. I'm not a scholar, just an ordinary man who perks up when he meets an extraordinary idea. But I know enough not to get hooked on any splinter of a traditional religion, cult, guru, or some charismatic evangelist.

Theosophy enriched my life with universal spiritual ideas that opened new vistas of understanding to make life more intelligible, meaningful, and enjoyable. The following represents some of ideas, in thematic format, to focus on insights that stirred my spiritual imagination.

WHOLENESS does not put money in the bank or assure personal salvation. But if you stop to think, not for a few fleeting moments but for a relaxed period of time, one comes to realize that everything within the Universe is interrelated and interconnected in an orderly, unified way. If not, everything in the Universe would fly apart and disintegrate. Just as the organs of our bodies depend upon each other for their mutual existence, so all the entities within the Universe – its organs – are interwoven into a "wholeness" for their mutual protection. The more we understand and feel the truths of this universal fact, the more we see the folly of fragmentation as compared to the benefits of cooperation. The world's concern with ecology, the environment, global warming, and so on, is really the slow awakening of the stupendous importance of understanding the concept of "wholeness." When we do, we'll know why universal "wholeness" is more spiritual than particularized religious Holiness. Accepting the concept of "wholeness" helps us to understand and appreciate the role of diversity. "Wholeness," in short, is wisdom. With it we see more, comprehend more, enjoy more.

SCIENTIFIC EVOLUTION has thrust us into a new way of looking at our human progress. Creational religions have evolved us out of heathenism, but now a new phase of spiritual evolution is challenging us to advance beyond creationism. New Thinking is following in the footsteps of the brave scientists who, centuries ago, challenged religion to change its belief that the sun revolved around the Earth. With physical evolution generally accepted as a fact, we can no longer plan our destinies based on past religious assumptions. Instead, we must explore how we can enrich our lives viewed from a new spiritual wisdom; for example, the plausible option of reincarnation which is a more logical conjecture of eternity instead of a life of perpetuity in heaven. Evolution is not just a pedantic theory, but a vibrant conviction that has vitalized and propelled spiritual evolution. It's as much a future Kingdom of God, as heaven is for the most devout creationists.

The new wisdom of SPIRITUAL EVOLUTION puts the spotlight on the main reasons why there's so much human misery in the world. There are two basic explanations why we have less-evolved and more-evolved people. First, there are young souls and older souls. Not all human souls were formed and began evolving at the same time, so that the older ones have had many more incarnations than have the younger ones. And second, we can logically surmise that some human beings made greater efforts to evolve than did others. We can see it clearly in our midst. So, during the last 5,000 years, the older souls – who also made greater evolutionary effort than the younger souls who made little effort – attained greater strides in spiritual development. The younger souls who made little effort to evolve are creating most of the havoc on earth. This is a quick but basic answer to those who are perplexed about why there are savages and saints living side-by-side on planet earth.

The intellectual basis of REINCARNATION was formed by ancient seers who noted the obvious differences between what they called the group souls of minerals, plants and animals – and the individualized souls of humans. As the mineral evolves into the plant, and the plant into the animal, the group soul evolves also from the mineral to the plant to the animal. Then, these seers claim, from among the most evolved animals, a few animals will split off from the group soul and evolve into primitive man with an individualized but primordial soul. These Homo sapiens evolved into Neanderthal, then Cro-Magnon, and then into the civilized men and women we are today. Our individualized souls not only remember the capacities we inherit from previous lives, but some of us remember the actual details of past lives. And as our souls take greater charge of our lives, the few will become the many who will remember in greater detail their experiences of past lives.

One hundred years ago, UNIVERSAL SPIRITUALITY was regarded as one of those ephemeral new religious ideas that come and go, but today millions are believing that the idea of Universal Spirituality is leading us back to the original concept of One Universal God. Seekers of new spiritual wisdom, and to some extent traditionalists, are beginning to see the colossal mistake religious leaders made. After many gods evolved into One God, they fragmentized the One God idea back to many religious gods. To their discredit, they were more interested in who was right regarding God, than in what was right. This blunder cost millions of lives, and the tragic divisions are still with us. At stake is the continuation of religious strife or the peaceful sharing of new universal spiritual wisdom.

SEEKING GOD'S GUIDANCE DURING QUIET TIME. Moses' Ten Commandments civilized the Israelites, Jesus' Kingdom of God converted the Romans, and Mohammed's Koran disciplined the Moslems. They asked for the impossible; their difficulties were enormous. Seeking God's guidance is as new and formidable an ideal to put into practice for our time as were the barriers of their times. Seeking God's guidance during a daily hour of meditation – It has changed the lives of thousands of people.

Religious wisdom is holding back the torrent of malevolence, for which we should be grateful, but its rite and rote are not powerful enough to stop it. A daily and intimate communication with God has a far better chance to elevate our human nature individually, and eventually collectively. Our challenge is to create new spiritual inspirational literature and massive grassroots discussion to show how we can find God in a new, more rewarding way. It will take a long time, but just imagine the kind of civilization we would have if most people would take personal charge in seeking

God's guidance rather than having the clergy digesting it for them. It can be done. It will be done. Perhaps you and I will meet in a future incarnation to enjoy the coming enlightened age where seeking God's guidance during meditation is the norm, rather than the exception.

COSMIC ENERGY GOD. Spiritual scientists are exploring new ideas to benefit our age in the way the prophets explored new values for their age. Using Einstein's cosmic science where he finds the noblest version of God, they add Cosmic Energy to the other designations – Spirit, Divine Mind, Universal Consciousness, as well as other versions. The new designation defines God as Cosmic Energy because it is the only entity that is ubiquitous, all-inclusive, all in all. Nothing exists outside of Cosmic Energy, or outside of God. It is total, as is God. And this spiritual Cosmic Energy has intention, purpose and cosmic super-intelligence to guide everything in the Universe.

When I breathe, think, walk or talk, it is Cosmic Energy that is sustaining and renewing me with a speck of its Cosmic Energy, as it is doing for all entities in the universe. When I seek God's guidance during my quiet time, God is there, as close as every thought and breath I take. There is nothing remote or abstract about my Cosmic Energy God. When an elevating thought enters my mind, I know it is my Cosmic Energy God communicating with me. Anyone who wants to make his life more interesting, more meaningful, more fulfilling, can experience it. You don't have to be a sage to comprehend it. All one needs is the willpower to persist in overcoming the initial failures in seeking God's guidance. A Cosmic Energy God is closer to us than visualizing God in a faraway heaven. Both refer to the same God. What's important is that we find the best way to listen to God's thoughts without the distractions that block God's "voice."

MAKING "HELPING ONE ANOTHER" THE MAIN PURPOSE OF OUR LIFE. Obviously, elevating our human nature to make helping people a world cultural religion is not going to happen soon. But it will eventually happen. First, it's already happening. People are helping each other on a far greater scale than at any time in history. The irony is that there is also more havoc in society, and people are also killing each other in greater numbers. Again, let me tell you why the "helping" ideal will prevail.

As human misery increases, those who have too much will eventually evolve into asking: "What for?" They'll begin probing for something more – as you're doing now. New Thinking will provide the answer. And those who don't have enough will find that the peaceful means to alleviate their plight will be achieved only through non-violence. Loving one another was asking too much, as religious wars have shown. But helping one another is more realistically doable, as evidenced by the fact that more and more people are finding that giving is more fulfilling than getting. Spiritual evolution is helping people discover the concept of "wholeness" through the ideal of helping others. Its practice has the universal potential to usher in the Messianic Age for which millions are waiting. If optimism is the oxygen of human progress, then I've given you a strong whiff of it. Breathe it in deeply!

UNCERTAINTY IS YOUR EVOLUTIONARY FRIEND. Uncertainty is the lifeline to human progress. Uncertainties deal with beginnings; certainties deal with endings. The unknown is the stuff dreams are made of, the raw substance of creation. The mundane uncertainties you speak of are the small learning struggles that are part of living. Life would be dull if we knew in advance the outcome of uncertainties. Columbus, Edison, and the Wright brothers would have lost their verve and fervor to seek the unexplored if they knew beforehand the endings of their beginnings. And to take this thinking a leap further, how would you like to know with certainty whom you're going to marry, the choice of your career, whether you're going to be a success or failure, and when you're going to die? To be bound to these certainties would be living the life of an automaton. Be grateful for the gift of uncertainty; it is what got us out of the caveman existence to the physical, mental, and spiritual civilization we enjoy today.

I was attracted to this wisdom because it provided answers to ultimate questions from above, and gave meaning to secular creativity below. From among the many secular insights that I gleaned from the new theosophical thinking, none intrigues me more than uncertainty. It is on the cutting edge of evolution, where the passion for adventure is laden with all kinds of possibilities and opportunities. The New Thinking from above inspired my secular thinking below. It dramatically changed the direction of my real estate career.

Chapter 13

Uncertainty Changed Me from a Caboose to a Locomotive

In 1955 my wife and I were attending a national real estate conference in Denver, Colorado. During the three days of sight-seeing, lectures and workshops, we were taken on a tour of the first newly built office building with the appropriate name of the Mile High Center. I was excited and impressed by its modern amenities of special flush fluorescent lighting, fast elevators, central air conditioning, thermostatically controlled heating, a beautiful marble lobby, and a host of other new office features.

My mind was already bubbling with an idea while flying home. "Honey," I said, "what would you say if I decided to build the first large new office building, like the Mile High Center, in Milwaukee?"

"I'd say, dear, give it a lot of thought before you plunge into a quagmire of uncertainties which I know you cherish, but which frankly, I fear. Milwaukee is not ready for such big a venture."

"I'm not going to jump in unprepared. When I do, the uncertainties will turn into what the Mile High Center did for Denver."

My mind was made up and my preparations began. My first concern was location. My basic plan encompassed a building of about 200,000 square feet with an attached parking garage of 250 parking stalls. I could not afford to buy and raze a square block of buildings in central downtown to accommodate my plan. I made a daring, unprecedented move. I bought a vacant square block of land two miles west on Wisconsin Avenue, Milwaukee's central thoroughfare, for $300,000. I hired a brilliant 28-year-old architect, Robert Rasche, to draw plans for a 185,000-square-foot building with 250 adjoining parking stalls. Armed with plans and beautiful colored renderings of the lobby and several exterior shots of the building, I set out to obtain a $3,000,000 mortgage.

My financial plan was based on these projections: a $3,000,000 mortgage with a 30-year amortization at 4 percent would come to a payment of $150,000 a year. All operating expenses I projected at $300,000 a year, the rent at $4.00 per square foot for 150,000 net rentable square feet at $600,000 a year, leaving a cash flow of about $150,000 a year after debt service and all operating expenses.

My net worth at this time was the free and clear: the $300,000 lot I purchased for the office building, $200,000 cash and a 24-family apartment building worth $200,000.

I knew the residential mortgage market, but I was a neophyte in the upper brackets of the commercial lending field. I was turned down by a half-dozen savings and loan companies. One of their executives summed up my chances with, "The largest loan ever made by a local savings and loan was $300,000. You haven't got the slimmest chance to get your loan here. Your only hope, and that's a slim one too, is interesting an insurance company in New York." After conferring with John Butcher, my banker, he agreed that an insurance company was my only source for a $3,000,000 mortgage.

Armed with my plans, pictures, and accompanied by my young architect, we flew to New York. We managed to see the financial officers of Aetna and Prudential. Each one asked the same question. "What corporation would be signing the mortgage?"

"I only represent myself," I said.

"Then we're not interested."

We tried others and got the same response.

As we were flying home, I compared my enthusiasm while flying from Denver with my drained hopes for my project. My optimism about uncertainty was taking a beating.

Mutual Savings and Loan was the largest in Wisconsin and it was run by 85-year-old Joe Crowley, and 90-year-old John Monahan. I got an idea based upon one of my New Thinking insights. I asked for an appointment with one of them and was turned down. I persisted, and a week later I was in the presence of the two elderly gentlemen. After delivering my memorized sales speech for a Mile High Center in Milwaukee, I ended with, "You and I know that we humans are at our best when we try to emulate God's process of creation. That's what inspires me to build the first modern office building in our city, and I hope you'll be equally inspired to creatively use your money and my work to make it happen."

I could tell that the last appeal created a wiggle of interest on their faces. They removed their hearing aids and Joe Crowley said, "Young man, you've got a lot of guts, but you also make a lot of sense. It's a daring project for you, and a big loan for us. Come back in a week and we'll give you our answer."

A week later I was waiting for my boon or doom when Joe and John walked in.

Joe again was the spokesman.

"We've done a lot of thinking and here are the terms under which we'll lend you the $3,000,000 amortized on 30 years at 4 percent. If you do not lease 50 percent of the building within eight months we'll step into your shoes as owner and complete the building and leasing as long as it takes. In addition, we checked and found that you own a 24-family building on Wisconsin Avenue. We want that as additional collateral for our mortgage. In short, you lose the $300,000 value of the land and your building, for a total of $500,000 if you don't meet our terms. They're tough, but we have to protect our investors."

My mind reeled for a moment. I swayed between no loan or a dangerous loan that involved the potential loss of ownership and the loss of $500,000, my total net worth. The uncertainties were mounting, but so was my momentum to go ahead. They watched me ponder their offer. "Gentlemen, it's a hard choice but I've made my choice; I accept."

Time was becoming a key element in my venture. Within a month, I let the three main contracts, Hunzinger Construction Co. for the building and parking structure; The Grunau Co. for plumbing; and Pieper Electric for all electric needs. When news of the project hit the papers, I was told by a few of my friends that Milwaukee wasn't ready for such a big change in office demand, and several savings and loan executives joked that Joe Crowley and John Monahan made the loan out of senility, not out of prudent business sense.

Now the crucial work began. I set a goal of making a minimum of 10 calls a day, concentrating on the upper echelon prospects – insurance companies, physicians, attorneys, accountants. Within a month I aroused a lot of interest, but no signatures. The resistance was typified by my first cousin, Dr. Joe Stone, an orthopedic surgeon, who, with his three associates, agreed on a functionally designed 4,000-square-foot office suite, but would not sign a lease because as Dr. Stone put it bluntly, "George, I'd love to move into your modern building, but what if for some reason you can't complete it, and we've given notice to our landlord to move out on a certain date, and we've got no office to move to? George, I'm a conservative guy, I don't take chances like you do. When I know for sure, you can count on my 4,000 square feet."

Mutual of New York, Prudential, Zurich Insurance Co., and several others showed interest, but viewed the project with the same skepticism my cousin did. There was one glimmer of hope. The manager of General Motors was enamored with the 10,000-square-foot suite my architect designed for him. "George," he said, "your building has got everything I want. I'm ready to sign a lease, providing you get an okay from my boss, John Nelson, in New York. Don't call him on the phone. I suggest you see him personally. I'll call him to give you my support."

Two days later my architect and I were waiting in John

Nelson's office. A kindly looking middle-aged man invited us into his plush inner office, where one wall was covered with a map of our 50 states dotted with many colored pinheads.

"Well, gentlemen, I know why you're here and what you're up against. Tell me why I should take a chance with an untried developer who's never built an office building before. You see those colored pins on the wall, almost all of them represent office suites leased in a building owned by a bank, insurance company, or a seasoned developer. My job is not to make a mistake that would embarrass my company and discomfort the 80 people who work for us in Milwaukee."

He listened politely and did not interrupt me as I put the most optimistic light on my venture, and ended with what I had dinned into my mind in preparing for the meeting. "Mr. Nelson, somewhere in the dim past, General Motors must have had situations where its future depended on peoples' help, where financiers took a chance on G.M.'s future. Taking chances is the life-blood of capitalism. It thrives on risk. If you take a chance on me, a speck of capitalism will thrive, because if you sign, others will sign. You'll burst the waiting of hesitant prospects. Do for me what others may have done for you."

I saw the same sign of yielding that I noticed on the face of Joe Crowley when we discussed the spiritual ideal of humanity imitating God's creativity. After asking a few more questions, he got up from his chair and detonated a capitalistic bomb when he said, "I'll sign your lease, but work like you've never worked before, because I don't like to make mistakes."

I flew home on air, both literally and figuratively. Within days I placed a quarter-page ad in the *Milwaukee Journal* in bold print reading: "There are Good Reasons Why General Motors Is Moving into the Bockl Building."

Within several months, Mutual of New York, Prudential, Zurich Insurance Co., and several others, including my cousin,

Dr. Joe Stone, signed leases.

My building was 35 percent leased and I had another four months to reach the 50 percent mark. The Kohler Company of Kohler, Wisconsin, and its labor union were embroiled in a bitter strike while I was negotiating with them on a 5,000-square-foot first-floor showroom. They were as anxious for the space as I was to have them. When they signed the lease, their attorney said, "Of course we expect you to use Kohler fixtures." It was an innocuous business request to which I did not object, but it flared up into putting me into a vice-like lose-lose predicament.

Two labor union men who were involved in the Kohler strike, walked into my office one afternoon and one of them, in a gruff voice without any preliminaries, said, "We're here to warn you that if you install Kohler plumbing fixtures in your building, we'll picket and shut you down." And they left.

I was boxed in on both sides. If I used Kohler fixtures and they shut me down, I would be disrupting the moving-in dates of the signed leases I had. But if I didn't use the Kohler fixtures, they might find reason to renege on the lease, and I would not only lose them, but also a satellite branch of the Marshall and Ilsley Bank that was interested in a ground-floor space alongside Kohler. I was in a serious jam, and during one of my quiet times, an ambitious plan formulated in my mind, based on the plot in "The Forgotten Factor," the play I had seen depicting how Moral Rearmament idealism solved a violent strike similar to the Kohler one.

While the inspirational thoughts I remembered from "The Forgotten Factor" were hot on my mind, and fearing that they might cool off by waiting, I called Ray Majerus, labor's point man leading the strike, and attorney Lyman Conger, Kohler's leading spokesman, to have a private, secret meeting in my home. I told them that I had an unusual plan to settle the strike. To my surprise, they accepted, perhaps because they were aware of the Bockl Building's plumbing predicament, or for whatever reason I was not aware of. They had not met personally, but each had thrown plenty of vituperation against the other through the medium of Wisconsin newspapers.

They acknowledged each other with a cold "Hi" before they sat down in my living room, warmed by a log-burning fireplace. The first few minutes were awkward, but soon they locked into a discussion of the strike's issues, surprisingly without hostility. I stayed out of their conversation until Lyman Conger turned to me and asked, "What's your plan?" I welcomed the question because I preferred their initiating it, to my my breaking into their conversation.

I began with a concise but dramatic description of MRA, and then related idealism to "The Forgotten Factor," where I emphasized the similarities between the two antagonists in the play and my two guests. I saw a glimmer of a reaction on their faces. I had hit home. I then zeroed in on the main thrust of the reason for the meeting.

"The key to solving most disputes," I said, "is to find a mutual interest that is superior to self-interest. We can say with complete assurance that mutual interest brings us closer to God, where the win-win answers dwell, in contrast to self-interest that draws us away from God, where self-interest solutions end in lose-lose violence. If each of you seeks guidance to find mutual interest in your dispute, you'll be enlightened by the difference between what is right and who is right."

I was pleased at their interest in MRA. They peppered me with questions, and kidded each other with friendly jibes how the main characters in "The Forgotten Factor" applied to them. They thanked me for an interesting evening, and to my pleasant surprise, shook hands before they left.

But my quandary about whether to use Kohler plumbing fixtures was not solved. The Grunau Co. pressed me for a choice, based on their scheduled work. I wavered for a few days and then made a King Solomon decision. I ordered standard plumbing fixtures for one half of the building and Kohler fixtures for the other half and waited for the shoe to fall from either Kohler or the union. Every day without hearing from either one was a victory. A week passed, then a month, without a call. Three months later the strike was settled.

Whether the private meeting in my home helped in any way, I do not know nor did I try to find out. The settlement not only got me out of a formidable uncertainty, it also induced the Marshall and Ilsley Bank to sign a lease, and other hesitant tenants signed leases because of the bank's prestige. Within eight months I had 70 percent leased, and within a year I had 100 percent occupancy, with a waiting list of a dozen eager prospects. After a year of operation, I drew a cash flow of $165,000, after all expenses and debt service. My equity was worth $2,000,000 on an investment of $300,000. Without Theosophy's wisdom about uncertainty, I never would have ventured into the swarm of unknowns.

What I experienced catapulted me into a new direction of my real estate career. I developed a passion for pioneering the creation of new kinds of real estate in Milwaukee. With the first modern office building shepherded through the minefields of uncertainty as a successful test case, I was now ready to devote my full time to discover new uncertainties that lie hidden in the unknown. I arranged to transfer my residential real estate business to my former salesman, Joe Zilber, and launched into my new, uncertain secular adventure.

Chapter 14

The Thrill of Discovery

T here's a difference between the spiritual thrill of discovering a new revelation and the secular thrill of starting a first-of-a-kind business venture.

The spiritual thrill of New Thinking permeated my right brain, which activated a feeling of transcendence, of inner peace, and tranquility. The secular thrill of discovery, of taking chances, is an outer excitement that's more physically vigorous than delving into New Thinking ideas. I latched on to secular uncertainties because I did not want to become a New-Thinking spiritual dilettante quoting its ideals without testing them on the secular firing line of action. I became enamored by the idea that the wisdom of each reinforced the other. Working them in tandem became the foundation upon which I built the fusion of all my future secular and spiritual activities.

With these thoughts coursing through my mind, I set out to find a first-of-a-kind project where I could practice my concept of spiritualized secular work. During one of my quiet times, synchronicity did its work. It linked what I was looking for to what the elderly needed, but was not available.

Special real estate projects for the elderly were still in their infancy in the early 1960s. In Milwaukee they had as yet not been born. Building an apartment complex exclusively for the elderly, with special amenities to meet their needs, had all the interesting uncertainties I was looking for, as well as providing an opportunity to help people.

After giving the venture a great deal of thought, I bought an acre of land overlooking the Milwaukee River, surrounded by a

grove of trees in a quiet, secluded part of the city. I hired architect Robert Rasche to draw plans for a two-story 84-apartment building with 42 one-bedrooms and 42 two-bedrooms. The design called for each unit to have a veranda from which to enjoy the beautiful scenery. The artist's rendering pictured a U-shaped dazzling white brick building with black wrought-iron fenced-in porches, against the backdrop of the blue Milwaukee River and tall luxurious trees.

The special amenities I planned for the elderly were a small, fully equipped restaurant to be used exclusively by the tenants for meetings with their children, grandchildren, and friends, and to enjoy tenant parties. Also, a prayer room, library, working area for crafts, and two outside shuffleboard courts with benches for spectators. The rents would be 15 percent below market rate, $34 a month for the one bedroom, and $40 a month for two bedrooms. My financial plan was to invest $250,000 of my money and obtain a $500,000 mortgage to complete the $750,000 venture.

Although I didn't expect any problem in obtaining the mortgage, it was not easy. My friend Bob Crowley, from City Federal, turned me down; Security Savings did, as did several others; and so did my good friend, Al Kliebon, President of St. Francis Savings and Loan, who was a devout Catholic and a pillar of spirituality in our city.

"Why," I asked Al, with whom I had several religious discussions, "did you say 'No' to my loan? Isn't it for a good cause and isn't it a safe loan?"

"I agree it's for a good cause, but my Board of Directors does not think it's a safe loan."

"Why?"

"Because they think the elderly are not good risks as tenants, and they didn't like the $75,000 expenditures on the special amenities because they don't bring in any income."

"They're wrong on both counts. The elderly have pensions

and the special amenities are special rental attractions. Al, you and I have had many talks on religion. Can I be frank with you? Don't you think that benefiting people is just as important as praising God in church? Can't we judge this $500,000 loan on a spiritual as well as on a financial basis? It's a special loan, and it should be given special consideration."

"You're a persuasive fellow, George. I'll try again. This time I'll be on your side."

A week later I got a call from Al that the Board had approved the loan, and within a month workmen were pouring footings for the first-of-a-kind real estate venture. A year later, Riverwood, the name I chose for the project, was ready for occupancy. Within six months, Riverwood was leased 100 percent. Tenants came from their own homes and apartments, and some had lived with their children. The average age was 65. Half were couples, and the other half were widows and widowers. Only a few were in their 70s and 80s. Most of them were retired teachers, policemen, stenographers, plumbers, electricians, and homemakers.

The social camaraderie was beautiful to behold. I hired an active and attractive 65-year-old manager who was born and raised in the South, and whose pleasant southern accent gave her management an aura of class. Within months, several romances developed that provided fodder for pleasant gossip. The special amenities were cheerfully used, especially the restaurant and the two shuffleboard courts. They organized teams and the elderly spectators cheered them on with the child-like enthusiasm they had 50 years ago. A school teacher wrote a beautiful poem, "An Ode To Riverwood," and pinned it on the bulletin board for others to read about the joys of living among wonderful people in the midst of beautiful surroundings. Whenever I felt fatigued and needed a lift, I drove to Riverwood and spent a few hours with some of the tenants. The difference between the first modern office building project and Riverwood was that one gave me secular satisfaction, the other spiritual fulfillment. Both were vitalizing, but with a transcendent difference.

While I was in a fulfilling mood from Riverwood, Willard Downing, a professor of sociology from the University of Wisconsin-Milwaukee, came into my office one morning with an unusual request. After a few preliminaries he said, "George, dozens of infants are born to 14- and 15-year-old mothers who are living in tragic neglect without care, proper food, or knowledge of motherly nursing. The childish mothers and their infants are wasting away, forlorn and abandoned by society. One of my students is caring for four infants in the basement of a church from nine to five. She calls for them in the morning, cares for them during the day, and drives them back home to their mothers. We desperately need room for at least 50 such infants and that's where you come in."

"I've made Mrs. Chester of the Chester Department Store family aware of the infants' plight. She thinks she can raise about $400,000 to build a day care facility for about 50 infants. I checked the cost for building such a care center. It's one million dollars. I'd like you to find a vacant building, remodel it to house 50 children within our $400,000 budget. I'm aware what you've done for the elderly at Riverwood, and I'd like your help on the opposite end of the age line – the newly born."

The professor highlighted the need and the problem with great clarity. Since I was between projects, I accepted this interesting challenge – creating a million dollar facility for $400,000.

Finding a vacant building of the right size, the right location, and at a low price proved elusive. I checked out a half-dozen buildings and none met all requirements. One of my former salesmen suggested that I call the president of the Guarantee Savings and Loan, Mr. Safro, who had foreclosed on a bowling alley located on 27th Street and Michigan. It had been gathering dust for many years. The professor and I liked the location and its 20,000-square-foot size.

We bought it with Mrs. Chester's donations at the bargain price of $100,000; it had been previously foreclosed on a $500,000 mortgage. After I had a plan drawn by an architect at no charge, I called in all the crafts – plumbers, electricians, carpenters, painters, etc. – to bid their work at no profit, only enough to pay their workers. When I explained the dire need for the project, they all agreed.

A half year later, we celebrated the completion of a $1,000,000 school for $400,000. It received a small grant from the State, and with a dozen volunteers, 50 infants were cared for lovingly during the day and 50 mothers were instructed how to care for their babies during the night. It marked the beginning of what is now known as the Penfield Center. It expanded Professor Willard Downing's compassionate idea into new buildings and new services to a multi-million dollar social agency, one of the most prominent in Milwaukee.

My pro-bono work in changing a vacant bowling alley building into a thriving facility to give neglected infants a new lease on life, and volunteers a chance to express their compassion, gave me a new idea for pursuing my first-of-a-kind real estate venture. Our city was replete with old vacant buildings that were deteriorating into blight and losing money for their owners. Why not use some of these buildings with their old-world interior charm for my new secular ventures? The more I thought about recycling old buildings into new uses, the more sound the idea became. What appealed to me, in addition to its immense possibilities, was that no one was doing it. The benefits from restoring old buildings were enticing – reviving neighborhoods, providing modern work or living shelters in an old-world atmosphere, and developing potentially sound economic ventures. The key to this New Thinking was to match the right location, the right building, with the right use.

I drove by the six-story white brick vacant building on the

corner of Prospect and North Avenues dozens of times without paying any particular attention to it. Neighbors called the 80-year-old former storage building a big white elephant. But now as I was driving past St. Mary's Hospital, a block away from the big white elephant, my mind clicked onto an idea that spurred my imagination. Why not turn the old warehouse into a modern medical office building for doctors practicing at St. Mary's Hospital? I parked my car alongside the building and began mulling over the idea. Why not start a real estate renaissance, combining old structures with new infrastructures right here with this building? The logic, the location, the building, and the use were all adventurously and economically favorable. This was an ideal building to introduce a new form of real estate shelter in Milwaukee. That excited me as much as the profit motive. And I was mentally ready for the uncertainties that potentially lay ahead.

The next day I called Jim Callen, the owner of the building and an acquaintance of mine.

"Jim, how would you like to get rid of your big white elephant?"

"How? Who?"

"Me."

"You? What have you got in mind?"

"How about getting $100,000 for it, and investing it in land on Mayfair Road which I know you're high on, and for a good reason."

"Is that an offer?"

"Yes."

"We've just bought the white elephant."

I purchased a 60,000-square-foot steel and concrete structure for $100,000 – it would have cost $1,000,000 to reproduce it. I had no difficulty getting a $750,000 mortgage from Aetna Insurance Company on the basis of an expenditure of $1,000,000, including an adjoining parking structure for 75 cars. I hired architect Abe Tennenbaum, who had a knack of combining the old with the new, circularized all the doctors who practiced at St. Mary's Hospital, and launched an advertising campaign in the *Milwaukee Journal*.

The doctors liked the location, but they objected to having their offices in an old warehouse building. They were not impressed with my efforts to sell old-world nostalgia mixed with the latest medical office features. Six months of nibbles didn't result in any signed leases. The mortgage people were getting nervous, and suggested I rent to others. I leased 5,000 square feet to a sales company, but continued to concentrate on leasing to physicians. My adherence to the original plan paid off. A group of the leading surgeons of St. Mary's Hospital had shown enough interest for me to draw a detailed plan for a 7,000-square-foot suite. They liked it, but still hesitated.

The lead doctor asked bluntly, "How do we know that our suite will look as beautiful as you describe? Why should we take that chance?"

"With full respect for your profession," I replied, "wouldn't I be taking a chance when you operate on me? We take chances with your profession, please extend the same courtesy to ours. We take a chance with our lives, you take a far lesser chance."

After another 30 minutes of friendly conversation, they agreed to sign the lease. When the dozens of hesitant doctors saw the splendor of the glazed white brick after the grime was removed, the new entrance, the beautiful lobby and the surgeons' modern suite, one-by-one an ophthalmologist, an oncologist, an internist, and others got off the sidelines and signed leases. Within a year after completing the recycling, the Prospect Building, as I named it, was two-thirds leased to doctors and one-third to others. It would have taken too long and would have been too costly to fill it with doctors. The venture produced a cash flow of $50,000 a year after all expenses and debt service, a 20 percent return on my $250,000 investment. It proved to me and others that recycling old buildings to new uses was a sound economic effort on the real estate horizon of the future. Its uncertainties were filled with possibilities and opportunities.

Chapter 15

I Ride The Recycling Wave

W hile I was visiting the construction of the medical building, hippies who congregated daily nearby, voiced protests, and one of them summarized their complaints, "The Establishment doesn't give a damn about us who're out of it. You cater only to the rich to get rich. There's no money in catering to us; that's why you ignore us."

There was a daily drumbeat of these protests. The protesters were non-violent, and some of them were well-educated and spoke eloquently. I sympathized with their plight, I had been there myself, but it was too big a problem for me to do anything about.

During one morning quiet time, the hippie problem, which subliminally smoldered in my mind, caught fire. There was an abandoned auto sales and repair shop building across the street from The Prospect Building. The idea that hatched in my mind would help some of the hippies' plight, and remove a neighborhood blight. My thinking took this track: Because the auto building, with its 100-car parking lot, was in a densely populated area, might it not be feasible to convert it into a mini-mall of small shops? Some of the more qualified hippies could rent from it and thereby get a piece of the Establishment. The first floor of the former showroom area, and the lower former repair level comprised about 20,000 square feet. With a walkway in the middle, there would still be room for about 15 to 20 small shops.

The owner happily accepted my offer of $250,000 for the vacant auto shop and 100-car parking lot. But the local savings and loans thought it was an affront to their intelligence to ask them for a $600,000 loan for a project as bizarre as recycling an old, oil-slicked auto shop into as flimsy an idea as a mini-mall. However, the Richter Co., a mortgage broker, got an insurance company that judged the loan upon my track record with the combination of shops, parking and a densely populated area. It approved the $600,000 mortgage.

The remodeling project became the centerpiece of conversation among the neighbors who read the sign that the auto shop would be changed into a mini-mall. The area was alive with anticipation. And when I announced to the hippies and others that I was ready to sign leases, there was a flurry of interest. I threw financial caution to the wind, when I leased stores to Jack's Dirty Record Shop, Pants For Men Only, The Love Matchmaker, and an assortment of other unusually named ventures. The local savings and loans were right. Within eight months most of them failed, and I was left with only a few rent-paying tenants. My rental income was about $35,000 a year against an operating expense and debt service of $80,000 a year.

My entrepreneurial juices began flowing with ideas on how to close the gap between income and expenses. Satisfied that I had answered the call of the hippies, I geared up to get the project out of the red with the help of the Establishment. I got the Marcus Corporation interested in building two small movie theaters, followed by leasing 3,000 square feet to the Chocolate Factory restaurant across the mall walkway. The idea was to feed each other with customers. It turned into a good match; each profited from the other. Their success attracted leases from Video Visions as well as Thai and Greek restaurants. I raised the income to $100,000 a year.

My recycling innovation did not turn out to be a great financial success, but it met the needs of a densely populated area, replaced blight with thriving activity, and together with the medical building across the street, they rejuvenated a key corner of Milwaukee's east side.

The successful recycling of The Prospect Medical Building and the Prospect Mini-Mall created a slight stir as a viable approach to future real estate development. What I needed to give a more visible thrust, was to rehabilitate a name building that had fallen to low-level use and disrepair. There were four such buildings: The Cudahy, the Astor, the Pfister and the Knickerbocker. I chose the Knickerbocker because it was the most misused and with the highest vacancy. Its owners were four roofing-and-siding brothers – Jack, Irv, Oscar and Eddie Kaiser. I met Eddie at Brynwood Country Club and liked him. He was gruff and tough on the outside, but mellow on the inside. I could tell he tried and succeeded in being honest.

"Eddie," I said one day at lunch, "I want to buy your building. I've got a few ideas to change the mess it's in."

"You've got it right, it is in a mess but you'll have to talk to Oscar, he's the boss."

I knew Oscar by sight and when I sat down with him and Eddie in what was formerly a beautiful Knickerbocker lobby, it didn't take long for me to see that I was dealing with a sleek, shrewd operator.

"This was the most outstanding building in Milwaukee," he began, "and I'm afraid you may not like my price."

"What is it?"

"A million and three hundred thousand smackers."

"How much are you losing on it a year?" I countered.

"That's got nothing to do with the price. What gives it value is its potential." He argued shrewdly.

Instead of responding to his cogent reasoning, I said, "I'd like to walk through the building and then see some of your statements on income and expense."

"We'll be glad to show you the building, but we don't keep any records of income and expense. Eddie, give him a tour of the building."

As I inspected the large and small vacant apartments and a few occupied ones, I was somewhat concerned with the dirt and neglect, but much more interested in the beauty of the woodwork with the potential I saw for the new ideas I had for the building. I had a price of $1,000,000 on my mind, but when I walked through it, I upped it to $1,150,000. When we finished the tour, Oscar was waiting for us in the lobby.

"Well, Oscar," I said, "there are few buyers for a run down building that no doubt is losing money. My offer of $1,150,000 is far more than fair."

He must've felt my eager vibrations because he resolutely countered, "George, it's got to be $1,300,000 and not a penny less."

I felt his vibrations also. I knew he meant it. I put out my hand, "Oscar, you've got a deal, at your price." I couldn't stop the momentum of my interest.

I had no trouble obtaining a $1,000,000 mortgage from Bob Crowley of City Federal Savings and Loan. I bought three old vacant homes adjoining the Knickerbocker for $100,000 from my ebullient Italian friend Bill Calvano to provide parking for what I had in mind.

My basic plan for converting the Knickerbocker into new untried uses consisted of three parts.

Divide each of the some 35 large 3,000-square-foot apartments into four to five modern efficiencies. This would increase the number of rentable units to over 200.

Lease 60 apartments to elderly people 75 years and up, with a nurse on the premises to care for any health emergency. I would change one of the large apartments into a private restaurant area where I would provide three meals a day, and charge $350 a month for a single and $450 for a couple. Except for religious institutions, there was no such facility in Milwaukee.

The third part was the most innovative. I named the idea "Home Away from Home." I would set aside about 40 apartments and rent them by the week or month to actors who came to our city to put on a play for a week or more, to a family whose home was temporarily ravaged by fire, a professor who would come to lecture at one of our universities for several weeks, an executive who would come for several weeks of training for a new job, or an irate husband who, after a quarrel, decides to leave home to cool off for a week or two. For these and other reasons, renting a small suite by the week would be a money-saving attraction compared to renting high-priced hotel rooms by the day.

I figured my income from the 200 units would come from 40 suites of Home Away from Home, 60 suites from Assisted Elderly Living, and 100 suites from tenants who rent by the year. I had in mind a highly qualified couple, Judd and Lillian Post, two retired attorneys, to manage this unusual mix of tenants.

Within a year all my plans became realities. "Home Away from Home" idea took off immediately, and it took close to a year before I rented the 60 apartments to the elderly. And I had no problem leasing the remaining units to long-term tenants. The cash flow after operating expenses and debt service was much more than I expected. What rewarded me as much as the financial success, was what I saw going on among the mix of tenants. The elderly, who mostly came out of lonely situations, were hobnobbing with young actors and others who for various reasons were living temporarily at the Knickerbocker. In the camaraderie, the elderly were sharing their wisdom and the young their conviviality. Occasionally the transitory tenants invited their new acquaintances to Sally's Restaurant, a formerly bedraggled eating place in the building which Sally rejuvenated into a first-class Italian restaurant. In a few instances, the nurse had to call one of the elderly tenants' child or grandchild to help her put their father or grandfather to bed after he had too much to drink at Sally's.

The conversion of the floundering Knickerbocker was a huge success, a beacon for others to do the same and go beyond. My recycling venture may have influenced Ben Marcus to buy the run-down Pfister building for a million dollars and convert it to one of the outstanding hotels in the nation. John Bach and Jerry Hiller bought the neglected Astor building for less than a million and renovated it back to its original old-world splendor. They subsequently sold it to the partnership of Tom Hauk and John Creighton, who up-scaled the old-world apartments in an expensive melding of gracious nostalgia and efficient modernity.

The half-vacant Cudahy building was bandied from investor to investor who did nothing to utilize the treasures of its beautiful architecture, until Michael Cudahy, of the new generation of the Cudahy family, bought and recycled the landmark white building overlooking Lake Michigan into dazzling condominiums, each one a glorious wedding of today's glamour of the new with yesterday's charm of the old.

I'm a starter, not a star. The stars are the recyclers of the Pfister, Astor, and Cudahy buildings – investors who spent tens of millions of dollars to show the real estate industry that it's economically feasible to revive dying buildings to new useful life. The Knickerbocker was a mere rudimentary starter, just a forerunner.

My secular work did not interfere with my attending what I called the meditative school of wisdom. I pictured myself as being on a quest, not on a tour. I convinced myself that the secular and the spiritual challenge each other to accommodate each other. That insight greatly influenced my life. I had a clear vision of what it means to conduct oneself spiritually, ethically, or self-interestedly. Each produces different kinds of people. The spiritual are on a quest to tap into the unexhaustible wisdom waiting to be discovered with which to enrich their lives. The ethical use reason to fulfill their lives; and the self-interested get satisfaction from amassing wealth, wielding power, or gorging themselves with pleasures.

What's the value of thinking about these ideas? It's to enrich the right side of the brain where the visionary ideals gestate, and to give meaning to the secular left-brain activity so it doesn't become ant-hill, driven work. We need right-brain transcendence to avoid barren left-brain lives. The New Thinking right brain idea of seeking God's daily guidance has added a meaningful dimension to my secular work. It has enhanced my interest in meeting all kinds of people and enjoying, sharing, and illuminating our differences. Without right-brain thinking, my business successes would be exciting, but not inspiring. There's a big difference. Inspiration does not come by itself. We have to seek, and find the ideal before we can feel its transcendent vibrations.

The conjecturings of New Thinking sages that our imperishable soul, which leaves our perishable body, comes back for endless adventurous incarnations, gives me an optimistic, inspirational sparkle that atheistic oblivion, or living in heaven forever, did not. And when I asked a number of intelligent men and women why there is so much depravity and misery on earth, none came up with the basic New Thinking answer that spiritual evolution is only 5,000 years old compared to our physical evolution of hundreds of millions of years. That profound right-brain answer gives us an understanding, as no other reason does, of the difference between the spiritually evolved and the less evolved people in our midst.

But before I get carried away in my New Thinking polemics, I want to go back to practical reality by describing how secular ideas are just as welcome in right brains as spiritual ideals.

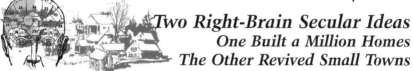

Chapter 16

Two Right-Brain Secular Ideas
One Built a Million Homes
The Other Revived Small Towns

One day, while I was still in the residential real estate business, Spike Kallas, one of my salesmen, walked into my office and said, "George, I've got a great idea."

"What is it?"

"Why not insure mortgages the way companies insure everything else. I've given it a lot of thought and I'd like to discuss it with you."

After talking about it for half an hour, I suggested he talk to Mike Frank, one of the attorneys who closed our real estate deals. Mike listened to Spike's idea and suggested that he should explain it to Max Karl, my brother-in-law, who was Mike's law partner.

The idea caught fire in Max's mind. As he explained it to me, after he thought about it for a few days, his plan was basically as follows. The Mortgage Guaranty Insurance Company (MGIC), the name he chose, would insure the typical $50,000 home for a fee of half of a percent of the $50,000 or $250. The mortgage company would either charge it to the buyer or absorb it. Insuring the loans would encourage mortgage companies to make 90 percent loans instead of the usual 80 percent loans, and thus increase the number of buyers with smaller down payments to purchase more homes.

Max, Mike, and Spike became the three owners of the company. Max took the lead. He took a hiatus from his law practice to spend full time in organizing and promoting MGIC. Mike spent half time closing deals and the other half helping Max. Spike divided his time between MGIC and selling homes.

It was a virgin insurance idea filled with technicalities, but

Max Karl was a brilliant lawyer who rose to the challenge of dealing with bureaucratic state insurance commissioners and presidents of mortgage companies. He was also a gracious, warm person, and a superb salesman. Max was an accomplished singer, and after dining with executives of mortgage companies in various cities across the country, he would sing his favorite, "The September Song," with as much passion as any of the popular professional singers did. Single handedly, within three years, using his legalistic knowledge, his persuasive selling ability, and his singing; he put MGIC on the national map.

Using reinsurance, MGIC built larger reserves with which to expand, and their profits soared. Seventeen years later, MGIC was sold to the Thompson Co., for $1,200,000,000, and subsequently, after some problems, it was acquired by Northwestern Life Insurance Company, where it is today. It was reported in The *New York Times* that MGIC's insuring of mortgages accounted for building a million more home ownerships. That's what happened when Spike's right brain and Max's left brain joined to make a colossal contribution to the real estate professions.

The other right-brain idea was equally spectacular, but on a state level as insuring mortgages was on a national level. During our occasional office discussions about social and economic issues, I would point out that nothing was being done to revitalize the small towns of Wisconsin. The earth would be a better place to live, I said, driving our discussion, and its population would be more fulfilled if more people lived in vibrant small towns rather than in huge megalopolises like Mexico City, Los Angeles and other overpopulated cities. I quoted social scientists who had made the analogy that when mice are forced to live in close quarters they become violent, and when they are given more room, they live peacefully with their neighbors. As with mice, so with men.

"So why don't we do something about it?" Jerry Berman, one of my top salesmen, volunteered.

"Like what?" I asked.

"Like building modern apartments in dozens of small towns of Wisconsin. I've been in many small towns and they don't have modern apartments. You like new ideas that benefit people. Well, here's one that will invigorate small towns by providing conviviality and comfort for the elderly who now live in large houses, and attract young couples to live in modern housing they can afford."

After a few days of barnstorming the idea, I decided to go ahead with it, prompted by my secular prudence that Jerry Berman was as capable of vitalizing small towns as Max Karl was of insuring home mortgages. To firm up the idea, Jerry got his brother-in-law, Jerry Shlensky, who had a university degree in light construction, to do the building of the apartments.

I structured the small town building company as follows: I would provide $100,000 for working capital and divide ownership; 60 percent for Jerry Berman, 15 percent for Paul Spector for supervisory managerial, and 25 percent for me as a silent but interested partner.

Jerry Berman was far more successful than I had anticipated. Small-town real estate brokers helped him find building sites, local public officials welcomed his ideas and helped him with permits, and small town savings and loans eagerly approved the apartment mortgages. Small-town newspaper editors praised the contribution we were making to their towns. The typical loan for a 16-family building was about $100,000; we built it for $130,000 and sold it to investors for $160,000. The tenants, as we anticipated, were mostly the elderly and the young. The elderly left the hard-to-care-for large homes and the young liked the modern facilities and the low rent. We built apartments in about 25 small towns. Here is a partial list: Fond du Lac, Appleton, Oshkosh, Clintonville, Sheboygan, Ripon, Lancaster, Fort Atkinson, Jefferson, De Pere and Watertown. In Ripon, Lancaster, Watertown, and Jefferson, we also built small motels.

The investor, who paid $160,000 for a 16-family building, years ago, can now retire on its income or sell it for about $500,000.

I claim little credit for Jerry Berman's unusual success in revitalizing Wisconsin's small towns. After a few years I sold my 25 percent ownership to Jerry, he didn't need my money or guidance anymore. When I took an occasional trip with Jerry and visited a few of the small towns to see what he had accomplished, I was rewarded with the same heightened fulfillment as when I used to visit the elderly in the Riverwood apartments. It was another exhilarating feeling – being on the cutting edge of the new and untried.

Chapter 17

Three Left-Brain Secular Solutions

I was disturbed to read that the Steinmeyer building was slated to be razed within a few weeks. It was vacant and supposedly a drain on the owner's pocketbook. I drove to 3rd and Highland and looked at its beautiful red brick and ornamental concrete trim, and then spent 30 minutes admiring its old-world woodwork as I walked through its interior. I enjoyed the coffee fragrance that still clung to its walls after decades of being the center of grinding coffee beans, distributing the aromatic coffee by horse and wagon to retailers. The horse hitching posts were still there, a reminder of its past. I bought the 50,000-square-foot building for $50,000 without knowing what I was going to do with it.

I got my right brain working and came up with this idea. There were mainly three grades of office space: A, B, and C. "A" space was centrally located, beautifully designed and leased at high rentals to high-priced attorneys, insurance companies, accountants, etc. "B" space attracted medium-priced attorneys, mortgage companies, and those who were aspiring eventually to move up to the "A" category space. "C" tenants, who couldn't afford "B" or "A" space, generally paid "C" rent but in neglected old buildings with poor services and in less than desirable neighborhoods.

The "C" tenants were the ones I had in mind for the Steinmeyer building. I would charge them "C" rents, but in a newly infrastructured building. Because I bought the Steinmeyer building at a low price, and recycled it economically, I figured that I would not only attract unhappy "C" tenants, but also a few "B" tenants who liked the newly restructured comforts, the lower "C" rents, and a location only a few blocks from central downtown. Within a year after I economically recycled the building, I filled it with "C" renters, and realized more than an adequate cash-flow profit.

I provided a new category in the office leasing real estate business that benefited lower strata earners with comfortable and modern office space that fit their budgets. It was a win-win-win situation for a dying building, for the neighborhood, and for tenants who were paying "C" rents in dilapidated "D" buildings.

The secular logic that went into the Steinmeyer building prompted me to find another, on the northwest corner of 7th Street and Wisconsin Avenue – a 100,000-square-foot building that was formerly an automobile showroom and repair shop. It was about 20 percent occupied with temporary use at negligible rents. Mr. Welch, its owner, was an elderly, wealthy industrialist who stuck to his unrealistically high $500,000 asking price, while the building kept deteriorating. Its location and condition lent itself to the same economic, secular thinking I used in the Steinmeyer building. The obstacle was the high price and Mr. Welch's steel will. I approached him with this deal-making idea.

"Mr. Welch, let's assume that you sell your building for $500,000. After Federal and State taxes you'd be left with about $300,000. If you invest it at the going 5 percent interest rate, you'd be earning $15,000 a year. I've got an idea where you can earn $20,000 a year."

"How?"

"By leasing the building to me for 50 years at $20,000 a year."

"You mean I turn the building over to you without a dollar of your money?"

"That's right, but you'd be getting $20,000 a year instead of $15,000."

"I've never heard of leasing a building for 50 years."

"It's a common practice to lease land or buildings for 99 years in New York and other large cities."

"I'm going to take your idea to my attorney at Foley and Lardner. He'll know what you're talking about and advise me if it makes sense."

A week later I was at his office again.

"My lawyer thinks you have an acceptable idea providing you agree to spend $100,000 during the first year of the 50-year lease."

"That's no problem. I'll probably spend more for what I have in mind for your building. Is it a deal?"

"Yes, it's a deal."

It took more time and more than the $100,000 to upgrade the old elevators, heating, plumbing and electrical infrastructure. But after extensive advertising, making hundreds of calls, hundreds of showings, I got the building 80 percent occupied and showing a 15 percent return on my $150,000 investment.

Among the interesting "C" tenants were the Milwaukee Bucks basketball team during their early formative years, the Steelworkers of America, and several law firms because the building was close to the courthouse. My left secular brain played the leading role in this venture, especially converting the $500,000 high price into a 50-year lease.

The third left-brain secular venture involved building a hotel in the center of the student residential part of the campus of the University of Wisconsin in Madison. The right-brain idea was concocted by two German refugees who bought a lot on Langdon Street for $25,000, and came to me for help to execute their idea. They offered me 25 percent ownership to spearhead the work. I liked the two partners. Gus Wand was a former salesman of mine, and Ernie Lane was a close friend. And I liked the hotel idea, especially because my two daughters, Bonnie and Judy, were students at the university, and when I visited them, there was no modern hotel in Madison where my wife and I could find comfortable overnight lodging.

The first major obstacle was to get the lot re-zoned from residential to commercial. With my partners at my side, I personalized my arguments before the reluctant zoning board with the inconvenience of having to stay at the antiquated Park Hotel away from the campus, when I visited my daughters. After a lengthy discussion about the many benefits of a new 100-room hotel, the board hesitantly gave us its approval.

My partners' architect drew a functional plan to hold the cost down to one million dollars. We took it to the Findorf Co., the largest building contractor company in Madison, and got a bid close to the architect's calculations. With this information, the three of us went to Anchor Savings and Loan, the largest in Madison, and asked for an $800,000 mortgage. They hemmed and hawed, but the reasons for the hotel's success were so persuasive that, after much deliberation, they okayed the loan. The main obstacle however, still remained – where to get the $200,000 to close the gap between Findorf's bid of a million and Anchor's mortgage of $800,000. Gus and Ernie did not have the money, and the only hope was for Findorf to take their probable 20 percent profit in the form of a $200,000 second mortgage.

The stakes against it were high, but so were the arguments for it.

We walked into the CEO's office and Gus and Ernie let me be their spokesman.

"Let me repeat for emphasis," I began, "what you probably read in the papers about the reasons for the potential success of the Madison Inn on the campus. The sources for its occupancy are indisputable – thousands of parents visiting thousands of students, campus conferences involving outside personnel, visiting lecturers, businessmen selling products to fill the university's needs, and Madison's general population who would be attracted by a new modern hotel. What I'm driving at, is for you to take what we assume to be your 20 percent profit of $200,000 in the form of a second mortgage to be amortized in five years at 6 percent interest."

"We couldn't exist very long by taking our profit in second mortgages," was the CEO's terse reply.

"But this is a special case. First, it's one of those 'can't lose' deals; and second, it's backed by the abilities of two exceedingly smart men who will operate it with more than ordinary efficiency."

"I agree that the Madison Inn will fill an obvious need."

But before he was about to offer another objection, I cut in with, "Then why don't you become a proud part of it."

"It's not what we usually do." I saw a bit of yielding, and I closed in.

"Without your help, the Madison Inn will probably be built by some firm in Milwaukee. Your choice is to earn nothing, or a prudent assurance that your $200,000 profit will be paid in full in five years, or earlier, at 6 percent interest."

We chatted for a bit longer, and then I got Gus and Ernie into the conversation. Their poise and intelligence, I could see, impressed him. They closed the gap against further objections, helped fill the $200,000 financial gap as well. Everything was a "go" on all fronts, and Madison Inn was built with $25,000 cash and the machinations of three secular left brains.

The hotel was an instant success. A year later, I stepped out with a small gain; but several years later, Gus and Ernie sold it for three hundred thousand dollars profit. It is now worth $3,000,000.

Because my secular ventures are used as news stories, I was invited to speak at real estate meetings and conferences. Among the various subjects I discussed, these four requirements for becoming a successful real estate developer had the greatest appeal. They are guts, imagination, persuasion, and integrity. I liken them to the four legs that hold up a table. If one doesn't have guts, if he fears the unknown, the uncertainties, then real estate development is not for him. If he doesn't have imagination, if his left brain can't conceive the details to form the potential outcome, then the table will wobble. If he can't persuade backers, with picturesque language, to see the benefits of his venture, then the table will wobble dangerously. And if he doesn't have integrity, if cutting corners and cutting the truth is given priority over honesty, then he not only short-changes his life, but also destroys the success of his project; the table doesn't just wobble, it collapses. The table analogy appeals to first-time real estate developers because it focuses directly on the core essentials for becoming a successful entrepreneur.

Chapter 18

I Publish Four Books on
How to Make Small and Big Fortunes

With the suddenness of a bolt of lightning, I received a jolt on October 20, 1963, that took all my spiritual resources to withstand. I received a call from Miami, Florida, that my son was killed in an automobile accident. The words stunned my mind, shattered in an instant all my dreams for his future. His student days at Miami University came to a sudden stop, and my mind to a sudden emptiness because my son was here no more. We wept for days, the flood of tears enveloping all the "might-have-beens" for Bobby's life.

What helped heal my wound was a letter from a reincarnationist friend who wrote, "Your Bobby is launched on a new beginning, and after his soul's sojourn on the astral and mental planes, it will reincarnate in another body where it will meet new challenges and experiences to refine into spiritual wisdom. Your son is on an endless evolutionary journey, where his destiny is eternity. How much happier all of mankind could be if it viewed death as a gateway to a new beginning."

My friend strengthened what I had already believed. On a human level, physical separation strikes a stinging blow to the mind, but the reincarnational view helps it to accommodate and live with loss. The reincarnational view, with its optimistic equanimity, helped me to accept my loss.

Several months after my son's death, I received a midnight call from my 94-year-old mother that she wasn't feeling well. Fifteen minutes later, when I opened the door to my mother's home, her live-in elderly companion shocked me with, "Your mother is dead."

With tears running down my cheeks, I took my mother's hand and a flurry of thoughts rushed through my mind: clinging to her security after my grandfather died, the frightening night ride in a wagon of hay while crossing the border from Minsk to Poland, living precariously in Warsaw; waiting for our visa in Volomin; her agonizing sea-sickness on the bottom of the ship while crossing the Atlantic. And in America, where I watched her hidden anguish as she silently held back her tears, sharing the trauma of my aimless walking the streets with nothing to do, and the joy on her face when I became successful.

And most of all, I felt a rush of gratitude for her bravery in overcoming so many obstacles to give me this wonderful life in America. As I gazed at her face, I felt anew how she showered me with unconditional love, how she made me the center of her life. Moses' Ten Commandments gave her strength of character which she poured into me. She put me on a rock of security upon which I was now building new universal ideals for my own spiritual evolutionary quest. I owed her so much. Without her valor, my life would have taken a different turn. I would have remained in Russia and probably been killed at an early age.

My life now took another sharp turn, triggered by a request from Prentice-Hall Publishing Company to write a book on real estate. It evoked two strong feelings in me: my love for writing and the more overwhelming one, my desire to help people succeed in real estate. The latter stemmed from my gratitude to America for providing the opportunity and freedom for me to succeed. The written word had played a major role in my evolutionary progress. Why not write a book, or a series of books, to help others the way books had helped me? There was not much literature circulating nationally on the subject.

In preparation for writing the book, I bought an 80-acre wooded area in the Kettle Moraine district near Holy Hill. I planned to walk there with my dog, Jet, two or three afternoons a week to formulate ideas for my writing. I do my best thinking while I'm in meditative walking.

I enjoyed getting back to writing, but now the motive was different than when I had engrossed myself in writing the Russian novel. Then it was for earning money and self-aggrandizement, normal for a 24-year-old, but now my writing interest was not for money or aggrandizement, but for a desire to help people succeed in their real estate careers. I decided to direct my efforts toward the average person in or out of real estate, not to sophisticated tycoons who knew more than I. I planned to make it simple and clear with convincing detail as though I was speaking directly to each reader. After several phone conversations with the editor at Prentice-Hall in New Jersey, we agreed on the following title: *How to Use Leverage to Make Money in Local Real Estate.* It was a good title because it appealed to readers like the salesmen I recruited for my residential real estate company.

My walks in the woods were sacred to me. When I began them, my mind flooded with examples, phrases, and lessons, but always the practical secular was uppermost in my thinking. I explained the meaning of leverage with an unusual story I heard from a man who happened to sit next to me during a two-day seminar in Chicago on "New Ideas In Commercial Real Estate." He was from a mid-sized city and spoke with a foreign accent. He joined me at lunch and the first thing he said was, "I can buy and sell all those expert lecturers on the podium."

"What do you mean?"

"I make more money than all those guys put together."

"I'd be interested to know how you did it."

I could easily tell that my companion had a big ego. He didn't need any urging.

"Do you know the meaning of leverage, how to use it in real estate?" he asked. Without waiting for my answer he hurried on to tell me, "I now earn $500,000 a year on 35 leveraged small projects."

"Please explain your leverage theory, and then the detail how it worked in your 35 small projects."

"First the theory. You can't make refrigerators without knowing the theory of refrigeration. The idea of leverage is to build, mortgage and lease a piece of property so that when you invest, let's say $10,000 of your money in the project, you have a cash return, after expenses, of $10,000 a year." He stopped for a moment to smile and joke, "Just one percent."

"How do you do it?" I asked with increasing interest.

"It's not very complicated, all you need is a lot of common sense. You look around and find a carpenter who has a son or buddy as a helper to work for a fair wage without the 25 percent extras that a big company adds on. And you do the same when hiring electricians, plumbers, masons, painters. That's your team of craftsmen who play an important role in my leverage theory.

"Now you look for vacant lots in good locations owned by people who don't know what to do with them, and therefore can be bought at low prices. The next phase is more difficult, but doable – finding prospects for small free-standing buildings. I solved it by making selective cold-turkey calls, as well as enlisting the aid of commercial real estate brokers who are always interested in earning commissions. The typical prospects are insurance companies, attorneys, doctors, stationery distributors, and many, many more.

"The last phase of leverage is the most interesting and creative one. I'm going to describe a typical example, which I, with some variations, used in all of my 35 small projects. Let's say I lease a 5,000-square-foot free-standing building to an insurance company at $30,000 a year net, to me, for 10 years. My total cost for land and building is $210,000. But using the prevailing value of land and cost of construction it's appraised at $235,000. Based on that appraisal a savings and loan agrees to a $200,000 mortgage. My yearly payments, with little variation are $20,000 and my yearly rent is $30,000 a year. That's how I earn $10,000 a year on my $10,000 investment. In a few cases, my cost in a similar project can be as low as $190,000, and the mortgage as high as $200,000, so that I wind up with $10,000 in cash, and an average of $10,000 a year. I call that leveraging to infinity."

I learned more from him than from the two days at the seminar. I searched my mind for new ways to get big returns on small investments. Here are a few examples among a dozen I described in the book. Buy a property with a 5 percent down payment from an incompetent or older owner who doesn't want to be burdened with management. Or if one finds a good deal, but the owner insists on 30 percent cash down payment, then find investors such as doctors or retired people who don't like the fuss of managing property, but would be willing to furnish the 30 percent cash down payment for half ownership if they find a trustworthy partner who would take complete care of management. I cite such partnerships where the silent and active partners make mutually profitable deals.

I devoted 75 percent of my book on how to use leverage to make money in local real estate, but in as many cases as it was appropriate, I wove in the success power of balancing the secular with a nuance of the spiritual. I stressed the rewards of practicing the double win of helping people and the fulfillment it brings when we enjoy the feeling that we are making a contribution to society.

Within a year after the book was published, Prentice-Hall sold 100,000 copies. Because of its national and international distribution facilities, I received calls from several parts of the country, and one call from South Africa and another from Japan. The content of the calls varied. Some expressed appreciation for the new ways of earning money; others posed a problem or an opportunity for a project and asked for my advice; and still others lauded the book for stressing patriotism, integrity, and spirituality.

Prentice-Hall asked me to write another book. We agreed on the title, *How Real Estate Fortunes Are Made*. I detailed some of my own ventures and cited examples of how fortunes were made by others. Here are two spectacular examples. In the lower part of Victoria Island across the bay from Vancouver, Canada, are the Butchart Gardens, one of the most beautiful scenic gardens in the world. It was formerly an open excavated limestone mine about 50- to 100-feet deep, an ugly 50 acres surrounded by woods and farmland. The wife of the owner of this neglected pit, who loved flowers, got some money from her husband to terrace the cavernous jagged hole in the ground, and built walkways surrounded by the most exotic, many-colored, fragrant flowers from the remote parts of the Earth – a veritable Garden of Eden. A restaurant and gift shop are at its entrance. Millions of people come to view this world-wonder every year, and it is said that the wife who turned blight into beauty has earned more money than her husband did from the limestone mine. I was there and walked the pathways, mesmerized by the colors and fragrances from around the world. It was a marvelous example of how beauty, benefits, and money-making combined into a win-win-win.

The other example was what I read about a gutsy man who bought an excavated mine on the outskirts of San Francisco for a pittance and started earning money out of it in the following three ways. He charged a fee per load for half filling it with trash, then charged another fee per load for filling the other half with dump-fill Earth. He compacted and covered the entire area with a foot of blacktop, and sold the ten-acre site to a real estate developer for a neighborhood shopping center.

How Real Estate Fortunes Are Made sold so well for Prentice-Hall that they asked me to write a third book. After several weeks of discussing the content and the title, the editor and I agreed on the title, *George Bockl on Investment Real Estate*. Each of the two previous books took a year to write, and this one took a half year longer because I devoted a lot of space to philosophizing on the role of real estate as a long time investment compared to all others (especially the stock market) because I focused on the creative fun of depending on your own work instead of depending on others. My right brain played a more prominent role in writing this book than in the others.

The fourth and last book I authored for Prentice-Hall was titled, *Recycling Real Estate, the Number One Way to Make Money in the '80s*. I described in detail my successes in recycling old buildings and cited other successful recycling ventures. Some of the outstanding ones were Pioneer Square in Seattle, Washington, where a huge landscaped clearing was surrounded with dozens of century old buildings thriving with picturesque mini-stores, antique shops and restaurants. Old buildings on the ocean front of Monterey, California, were imaginatively recycled; one of them went as far as extending its floor in glass over a small stretch of water. In Carmel, on the coast of California, the little shops in alleys between old buildings were more interesting than those facing the streets. In San Francisco, my wife and I wore ourselves out visiting the many shops and restaurants in one of the most extensively recycled areas of old buildings in the country. In Chicago, gutsy entrepreneurs tested the limits of recycling by converting an ice house that took months to melt its walls and turn it into modern apartments. And, of course, there's Soho in New York City, where rent is higher in the picturesque old buildings than in new ones. Recycling old buildings to new uses has become a new art form where architects and designers collaborate to combine the charm of old and the function of new into an innovative, architectural beauty.

The four books sold 300,000 copies, and my royalties amounted to about fifty cents an hour. But the creative thrill I enjoyed in writing them cannot be measured in money.

MY LIFE IN AMERICA

Chapter 19

Teaching to Make a Difference

B ecause of the publicity from my writing, the University of Wisconsin's Education Outreach asked me to teach a course in real estate to working adults one evening a week for 17 weeks. I accepted the invitation with some trepidation because I had never done this before, but after a few quiet-time sessions, I dissolved my concern and embraced the new challenge.

As I waited at the front desk for my first class of students, about 100 men and women straggled into a room big enough for 250. When they were all seated and quiet, I welcomed them, and as a starter asked them to give their names, occupations, and what they wanted to learn for driving long distances to get here. In the class were real estate salesmen, appraisers, city assessors, urbanologists, plumbers, electricians, and carpenters; the consensus of what they wanted was to learn how to use leveraging to make money in local real estate. Apparently, I surmised, most of them had read my first real estate book.

I was as eager to teach as they were to learn. I prepared two hours of material for each evening session, so that I would have something specific and helpful to say about how to get into real estate deals with little or no money. I made it my main theme in the ensuing 17-week sessions that I taught over the next four years. There was little lecturing, mostly discussion. After I introduced an idea, we clarified it with questions and answers.

During the ensuing sessions I dealt with dozens of subjects, and the leading one by far was the 10 ways to finance real estate deals. Some were familiar to them, others were not. The one that none had ever heard of was the multi-mortgage plan. This is the way I described it. Suppose a man who has worked in the resort business wants to build a 50-room resort, but doesn't have any money. Here is how it can be built. He locates an unusual site to assure its success and then proposes to the owner of the land, carpenter, mason, plumber, electrician, and furniture purveyor that after they all submit their bids to complete the resort, he would pay each one individually the principal and interest for their portion of the multi-mortgage. He sells them on the double benefit, that he provides them work at a fair profit, and they invest what he owes them in a portion of the multi-mortgage at the prevailing rate of interest.

I discussed ways to buy property with a small down payment, how to option property, how to borrow money, how to evaluate the possibilities of a venture, and how to finance a project. I focused on how to find run-down properties, which are often owned by ailing or retired owners. It offers a goldmine of opportunities, and I described it with a concrete example.

Donald Pollock, a 29-year-old attorney, came into my office one afternoon and said, "Mr. Bockl, I'm an attorney, but I think I can do much better owning and managing properties, but don't have any money. How do I get started?"

"Scrutinize the 'Real Estate For Sale' sections of the *Milwaukee Journal* for what looks like a good buy and then come back and I'll describe the next step."

He came back a week later and said, "I didn't find any buys that interested me."

"Do the same for a month and then come to see me."

A month later he came to my office and said enthusiastically "I found two good ones, but, as you know, I have no money."

"Find a retired doctor, businessman, attorney, or anyone who would like to invest in property but who doesn't have the time or inclination to manage property. Offer him the proposition that in lieu of his investing the cash down payment to buy the property, he would become half-owner and in addition receive interest on his cash outlay. That you would manage the property at no charge to the partnership."

He found a wealthy pediatrician, Ely Epstein, who liked the arrangement and Donald Pollock bought his first 16-family apartment building. At the end of the year, the doctor liked the cash average, and so did Donald. It was a win-win; both benefited. Using this partnership method during the next eight years, Donald bought millions of dollars of properties and became a millionaire. That story, and that subject, excited my listeners more than many of the other ideas I presented on how to get into deals without money.

During the course of my teaching, several students reported successes in creating deals by using the information we discussed during the evening sessions. A few were dramatic, where I played an indirect role. At one of the evening classes, I described the 24 Ivanhoe apartments, located near Prospect and North Avenue, and the man who owned them.

"The building is in shambles," I said. "The inside is dirty; the walls are full of graffiti, the plumbing doesn't work, the tenants are smart-alecks, and the owner is having a tough time collecting rents. The owner is elderly, frustrated and is anxious to sell the building. 'It's worth a lot more, he told me,' but I'll take $250,000.' I'd like to conclude with this additional fact; the building needs at least $75,000 to put it back in normal rentable shape. Any ideas how to get into this deal?"

No one raised a hand. But at the end of the session, as the people were filing out of the classroom, Bob Pritchet, an electrician, stopped at my desk, "I qualify to buy the Ivanhoe," he said, "for two reasons, I have no money – the stuff you've been teaching us – and the second and better reason is that my son, wife, brother and I are a team that can fix up the Ivanhoe without the need to borrow $75,000. I'd like to buy it."

He struck me as a practical, hands-on type of guy who might be the right one to buy the building. I went to my friend, John Butcher, President of City Bank, described the deal, and asked for a first mortgage of $150,000 for Bob Pritchet and his team of helpers. He okayed it, and with a little persuasion I got the owner to accept a $100,000 second mortgage.

Within a year, Bob Pritchet and his family completely remodeled the apartments, replaced the unreliable tenants with more responsible ones, and doubled the rent. He was clearing $50,000 a year above all expenses. Two years later, Bob called me and said "Teacher, I want your advice about buying the next-door properties owned by some big company in the east. Except for a corner drug store that's rented, all these other properties are vacant and going to pot: the Oriental Theater, eight stores, a huge bowling alley and bar, and a nearby parking lot. What do you think I should offer for it?"

I was familiar with the neglected properties and knew that they were owned by Loewi Co., headed by the wealthy Tish brothers who were too busy to pay attention to their dilapidated real estate. I advised Bob to offer $350,000 with a $50,000 down payment. They accepted, and within three years Bob had all vacancies replenished and leased. Today, Bob and Dick, his brother, are millionaires. With inflation and excellent management, they are now netting about $500,000 a year from all their properties. It all started in a classroom where a $35-a-week electrician was bold enough to get into a big deal with no money.

Another unusual deal involved a restaurant, located on the corner of Lake Drive and Brown Deer Road. It failed four times under different owners. It was failing for the fifth time under the ownership of a Kohler, a most prominent family name in Wisconsin. He was a gracious host, and I got to know him well. I liked him more than his food. He bought the restaurant as a lark, to keep busy, and he was losing $75,000 a year.

George Pandl at the same time was having a different problem. He was a partner with his brother Jack in a restaurant in Whitefish Bay that had a seating capacity for 100 diners. Each partner had grown children and neither earned enough money to support their large families. George Pandl must've heard somewhere about my interest in getting people into deals with little money. One day he came to my office and described his problem.

"I could scrape together about $10,000," he told me, "and that's all."

Favorable synchronicity was on his side. Immediately the Kohler restaurant sprang to my mind. I went to my bank friend, John Butcher, and arranged a first mortgage of $150,000, and I had no trouble getting Kohler to accept a second mortgage of $75,000 after I profiled George's long experience in his family's Whitefish Bay restaurant. I suggested that Kohler not ask for the $10,000 down payment because George needed it badly to clean it up and make some changes. As the reader might suspect, the restaurant became an immediate success. But that's not all. His oldest son, Jim, a culinary major in college, assisted his father to turn the five-time "loser" into one of the outstanding restaurants in the state of Wisconsin, reputed to be valued at $4,000,000. The Pandl story gives proof to one of the truest real estate aphorisms: someone's problem is another's opportunity.

Another unusual money-making story deals with converting a $6,000 a year income into a $35,000 a year annuity for 30 years. One day a man called from either Pittsburgh or Columbus (frankly, I don't remember) and told me that he had read my books and would like my advice on a problem that was perplexing him. This, in substance, was his problem. "I'm a 60-year-old attorney. I own a building with a bank as the only tenant. It's in very bad condition, but the bank likes its location and is offering me $250,000 for it, probably $100,000 more than I could get from others. They're planning to spend $75,000 to remodel it into a first-class bank building. But I hesitate to sell it because after paying $100,000 in income tax, I'd be left with $150,000, which invested at 4 percent interest, would give me an income of $6,000 a year. How can I increase it?"

As he was talking, my mind triggered an idea.

"Listen carefully," I said. "If I get off the track call me on it. Here is what I suggest you do. Tell the executives of the bank that you're not interested in selling the property, but you would do the following to satisfy their need for the location. You'd be willing to borrow $750,000 at 4 percent from their bank and modernize the building as per the bank's specifications. Then adding the $250,000 worth of the building, you'd be willing to lease the $1,000,000 remodeled structure at 7 percent or $70,000 a year for 30 years, and at the end of the 30 year term, the bank becomes the owner of the building. Stress that point hard because that could be the clincher of the deal.

"Your payments on the $750,000 loan from the bank at 30-year amortization would be about $35,000 a year, and your income on the lease $70,000 a year. Your $6,000 a year income upon selling the building would be converted into a 30-year $35,000 annuity. It's certainly a good deal for you, and just as good for the bank, because it has a solid $750,000 loan on the books, it has the location it wants, a modernized bank, and ownership at the end of 30 years. Please call me in a few weeks. I'd like to know whether the bank liked the plan."

"Thank you very much. I think it's a great plan. I'm going to give it my best. You'll hear from me."

A month later he called, "With minor variations the deal was closed as you outlined it. You've turned my yearly income from $6,000 to $35,000. I'm very grateful. I'd like to pay for your valuable advice. How much do I owe you?"

"You owe me nothing. I owe you thanks for providing an interesting story which I'll use in my next real estate book."

During all the years while I was writing and teaching, my interest in new spiritual thinking kept murmuring in my blood. And now, with my writing and teaching real estate coming to an end, my urge to do something significant about my ideas came to the fore. With a predisposition toward action, and not prone to be modest, I was emboldened to think I knew enough to write a book about New Thinking Universal Spirituality for these two reasons: to clarify my own thinking, and perhaps to stimulate others to what I believed were treasures that enrich the soul.

MY LIFE IN AMERICA

Chapter 20

I am a Speck of Spirit Materialized Into Man

M y notions of God had been transformed and clarified from the vague man-image "God in heaven" to a Cosmic Energy God, whose body is the universe materialized into constellations, suns, planets, mineral, flora, animals, and man. In essence, I am a part of a God that guides and renews me, whether I'm aware of it or not. And what I've discovered is that the more I am aware of God's guidance during meditation, the more this Cosmic Energy God pervades my consciousness with life's understanding and fulfillment. This vision of God has opened vistas of new spiritual thinking, especially when I became aware that every thought and breath I take is the Cosmic Energy God, illuminating and renewing my mind and body.

I titled my first spiritual book, *God Beyond Religion*, where I concentrated on the obvious fact that divisive, dogmatic religions were responsible for mindless wars and millions of deaths. I naîvely failed to extol the virtues that the religions had planted in civilizing the world.

Through interviews, I profiled the attitudes of several categories of people in and out of religions. These are the paraphrased essences of their responses.

Ultra Orthodox: "Today's new thinkers are like the false prophets that spring up at every age. They want to change the old for the new. But God's original, pristine wisdom has no expiration date. All they do is sully the true with the false."

Average Traditionalist: "I don't bother with the far-out new spiritual thinking. I'm too busy with my own practical affairs. I'm content with the wisdom of my own church and religion."

The Average Person Out of Religion: "I don't miss the imposed rules of religion, but frankly, neither do I have something big to live for like those who are within religion. I also admit that many of us out of religion end up in addictions that trample on freedoms, and generally end up in self-destruction."

Ethical Humanists: "Human reason and ethical conduct is all I need to lead a good, fulfilling life."

A Self-Disciplined Person: "I'm opposed to imposed religious discipline as well as the absence of discipline. I definitely do not deny what is generally referred to as God; on the contrary, I want more of God, a more intimate and more believable God, a God to guide my life. I want a God to give me the open-mindedness to respect the traditionalist churchman's beliefs, and want them to respect my church with a membership of one."

I found right-brain spiritual writing much more difficult than left-brain secular writing. While probing the vast unknown was exhilarating, it was also fatiguing and full of doubts. My personal spiritual evolution is still in its infancy. God Beyond Religion sold less than 500 copies, but it did not discourage me from starting another spiritual book titled, Living Beyond Success.

The main theme of the book asks the questions, "What's the challenge to living beyond success? Is it to pile on more layers of success, or is there something intriguing, that when added to more success, makes its continuation more meaningful and fulfilling?" My answer comes from personal experience and from watching others who have that "something" and those who do not.

During the 1950s when I was suffused with secular success-es, I subliminally detected an ennui creeping into my psyche – a questioning of what was the meaning of all my successful striving. As I look back, that's why Moral Rearmament intrigued me; and later on, Theosophy. They launched me on a spiritual quest that not only subdued my ennui, but also invigorated my secular work.

When I discussed what I had discovered with some of my

intelligent friends, they said in effect, "George, you're making too much of a big deal about spiritual New Thinking. Reason and common sense, and a little whiff of religion, can get you there without all the New Thinking fuss."

"Do you equate common sense with spiritual sense?" I asked.

"With some improvisations, yes."

"Can reason and common sense stop a Hitler, a Stalin, a terrorist or a crooked businessman?" That's where the discussion ended.

Throughout the book, I tried not to sound like a sage giving advice, but like a practical, secular businessman who had experienced the ebullience of striving for success, but also had it reinforced with the thrill of spiritual inspiration. I tried to focus my writing on the importance of combining the secular with the spiritual, common sense with spiritual sense, so that we can actualize the full measure of fulfillment, rather than settle for the half measure of success.

In my third spiritual book titled, *Where Did We Come From and Where Are We Going?* I concentrate (with a lot more maturity) on the worldly fact of evolution and universal spirituality as the next evolutionary step beyond religious spirituality. After 5,000 years of spiritual evolution, we have evolved from barbarism, from many gods, from primitive tribes, to today's more civilized, more sophisticated religious organizations. But we have not as yet evolved from hurting and killing each other, and that's why we must embrace universal spirituality as the next evolutionary step for human progress. I stress that we should be grateful for what religions have done for us, but question why, with all the evidence of violence between religions, they are not seriously exploring the next universal evolutionary spiritual step?

I was criticized by many of my friends for touting universal spirituality because it was too visionary, and that traditional religions will never give up their cherished beliefs which had enriched their lives for centuries. My answer was that we wouldn't be enjoying today's wonderful freedoms had it not been for visionaries, hundreds of years ago, who took each evolutionary step to democracy from the entrenched feudal lords who ruled centuries ago.

The fact of evolution has given us the scientific answer as to where we came from, and universal spirituality is pointing the way to where we should be going. I'm not a scholar or a scientist, but an ordinary man who enjoys digging into the unknown where spiritual treasures are waiting to be discovered. What's enticing about it is that anyone can become a universal discoverer.

The fourth book, *A Conversation: With a New Thinking Sage*, with the subtitle, *How To Halt the Cultural Decadence of Our Age*, was my most ambitious attempt to formulate my new spiritual ideas from personal conviction. In the three previous books I treaded lightly, in this book I took bolder steps, asserting the differences between the old and new spiritual thinking with greater affirmation and delineation. These are a few of the persuasive insights for prodding new Universal Thinking from old religious beliefs.

Evolution is a fact that challenges the scriptural assumptions that were valid and valued for their times, but which are now no longer valid.

The mistake the religions made after Abraham's vision changed many gods into One God, was to re-fragmentize the One God back into many gods of many religions, with the violent result of killing millions. The goal of New Thinking is to give priority to a Universal Spiritual God.

The concept of Wholeness is that everything in the universe is interconnected, and that cooperation, as its natural law, not separation, is a spiritual advance over the concept of holiness. While holiness is a sacred feeling, it ignites emotions that lead to violence.

Our imperishable soul gathers wisdom or ignorance during our endless physical incarnations, each a distilled printout of its accumulated past experiences. This gives us a plausible conjecture about reincarnation that is more optimistic and believable than either living in one body forever in heaven or atheistic oblivion.

Teaching dogmatic differences within religions will continue to separate people into antagonistic flocks. Universal Spirituality must be introduced in the classrooms, not with the aim to dissolve those differences, but with the aim to learn from and to share the various religious wisdoms. When Wholeness is taught alongside religious traditional religions, new generations will thrive from enjoying each others' diverse wisdoms.

My most visionary insight, is that when the New Thinking is absorbed in world culture, we will elevate our human nature to a level where most of us will make helping people the main purpose of their lives. A small fragment of the world population is already doing it and experiencing inspirational rewards way beyond common experience. Teaching universal spirituality in the classrooms, and practicing Wholeness in human activity, could potentially bring us closer to the grand vision of living together in peace and harmony. Nothing is impossible in the advance of spiritual evolution!

Chapter 21

My Last Two Secular Hurrahs

During the years when I was writing, teaching, and exploring new spiritual thinking, I did not abandon my strong desire to remain involved in secular work. My pedantic interest did not slow; on the contrary, secular work gave it an extra glow.

At 70 I plunged into a recycling project that was replete with new challenges and uncertainties. In the central part of downtown, a hundred yards from the Milwaukee River, was a vacant, nine-story, 150,000-square-foot building, formerly owned by Klode Furniture. This store had been a long-time blight on surrounding commercial real estate. The owner tried to sell it for a million, five years later for half a million, and one day the owner's brother, Ralph Heilbrenner, came into my office and said, "George, you're one of the few who can find a use for it. Make any reasonable offer and I'll try to get it accepted."

A week later Ralph came to my office with an acceptance of my shamefully low offer of $200,000. I, like others, had no idea what to do with it, but my intuition told me that the building had the potential for a spectacular project.

While walking in the woods of my farm one day, I hit upon an idea that was as daring as it was new. The more I evaluated its uncertainties, the more intrigued I became with its possibilities. The first departure from the usual was to build 110 loft apartments in the center of the city where none had ever been built before. And to double the dare, I planned for each apartment to have a small store in front of its living quarters, just as small merchants like grocers and pharmacists did 50 years ago. And in the center of the typical 100-by-150-square-foot floor, I visualized an atrium of 35-by-75 square feet surrounded by 14 small apartments facing its street-like area, which I planned to "landscape" with flowers, benches, grass-like carpeting, and daylight lighting.

I knew I couldn't get a $3,000,000 loan for this anomalous project locally, so I went to the Federal Housing Administration Director, Larry Katz, and challenged him to be on the cutting edge of providing a new kind of living quarters by insuring the $3,000,000 mortgage. After I presented all my best arguments, and he all the objections, he reluctantly agreed to insure the loan. And after getting a variance from City Hall to combine residential and commercial zoning, the Chalet on the River, as I named it, was recycled to test all my risky leasing ideas.

The challenge now was how to get the attention of the unique brand of tenants. I got the art editor of the *Milwaukee Journal* to write a story featuring the idea that combining living quarters with a mini-store was a new art form of real estate shelter.

During the first six months, I leased about 30 of the 110 apartments to an interesting variety of people: a beauty shop operator, a semi-retired attorney, a florist, an artist, a jewelry craftsman, a photographer, and the most unusual one was a couple who joined two apartments and installed warm tubs where busy businessmen from nearby would come to relax in the soothing water and end the visit with a quick massage.

But my idea didn't succeed 100 percent. When I couldn't find more than 30 adventurous tenants, FHA stepped in and demanded that the rest of the apartments be leased to regular tenants. The Chalet on the River today nets a cash flow of $400,000 a year after all expenses and debt service. It was the star example for my book, *Recycling Real Estate: The Number One Way to Make Money in the 1980s.*

As I was approaching the age of 80, I became enchanted with the idea of waking up the Historic Third Ward from its 50-year slumber. Located three blocks south of central downtown, it was an area of about 10 square blocks of dozens of 100-year-old vacant manufacturing buildings. My motivation to make use of these old-world structures was my awareness that small entrepreneurs were operating from their basements because they couldn't afford to pay even the lowest downtown office rent.

I bought the 100-year-old, 120,000-square-foot Marshall Building in the Historic Third Ward for $350,000, and with a few amenities and window air conditioning, began renting space for as low as $3 a square-foot, a third of what office space was renting for even in ordinary buildings. They flocked to my building, and when they wanted a few more amenities, like carpeting and private offices, the rent went up to $5 a square foot.

A few ambitious small entrepreneurs wanted me to build modern showrooms for specialized businesses such as unusually designed furniture, a laboratory for manufacturing facial beauty products, a computer-related technological space, and other costly improvements for which the tenants had more dare than money. Remembering how people took chances on me, I risked spending about $1,000,000 to help these young business people get started in their careers.

The Marshall Building met a new need in an old neighborhood. When it was filled, I bought another 100,000-square-foot building two blocks away for $700,000, and spent $2,000,000 to recycle and lease it to the same type of tenants as in the Marshall Building. Together they began a real estate renaissance in the Historic Third Ward that has mushroomed way beyond my wake-up call into hundreds of apartments, condominiums, theaters, art galleries, and restaurants. The prices of old buildings quadrupled, and the Historic Third Ward has become the "hottest" thriving real estate area in the city. My two recycling ventures had created about 500 new jobs, and the others that followed created hundreds more.

My secular interests were as alive as my spiritual quest. However, because of my waning energies, I decompressed from creating new ventures to managing my four buildings: the Bockl Building which I had to take back for non-payment of a $2,500,000 land contract balance, my two Third Ward buildings, and the Chalet on the River. I was kept creatively busy, active enough to meet a $2,500,000 yearly payroll.

Chapter 22

The Challenge of Functioning at 93

My wife died in 1994 after being my dearest companion for 56 years of precious married life. Her absence left a wide gap of loneliness that was difficult to fill. Gone were the hugs and good night kisses, gone the small talk about the people we met during the day, and about our children and grandchildren, their problems and their triumphs. The mundane news we discussed was replaced by a deep silence. Eating alone became a chore, not the nightly delight it used to be. I discovered how clumsy I was in preparing simple meals. I took so many of my wife's dexterous little skills for granted, and now I realized how practical and important they were. We built our future together, we shared it together, and I was at a loss at how to live alone. I had to call upon all my spiritual resources to make the subtle changes with my family and work.

My reincarnational thoughts soothed my mind with the peace that my wife's death was a natural transition of the life-death-life cycle – generation, degeneration and regeneration. When I watched my wife take her last breath, and with tears rolling down my face, I said, "Honey, your soul has been launched on a new beginning." That poignant moment has remained indelibly marked on my mind.

My family of two daughters and four grandchildren has been of immense help in filling many of my empty hours. They invite me at least once a week to dinner, they include me in their family meetings and celebrations, and I receive one or two calls a day from one of the six to find out how I feel, and if there's anything I need. My grandchildren share their work and love adventures with me; they make me an active participant in their lives. I often remind myself how much joy I would have missed if I hadn't married.

I continue my secular work with the same entrepreneurial enthusiasm of long ago, except that I do it at a slower pace. But I'm still on the lookout for new ideas and new experiences.

While I was in the midst of my work, spiritual pursuits, and family involvement, a golfing buddy, Herman Williams, asked me if I'd be interested in meeting Adeline Shapiro. The name immediately struck a responsive chord. She was my first love; she had lived in the affluent Lake Drive area. When I was young I had been hesitant to propose because if she turned me down it would have lowered my already low self-esteem, and if she accepted, I was equally hesitant because I had no job or career to provide for a marriage. But that was 60 years ago. In the meantime she had married, had five children, a dozen grandchildren and a few great grandchildren. Unfortunately, her husband died 35 years ago, and she worked many jobs to educate her children through college.

"You haven't seen her for 60 years," Herman urged, "Wouldn't it be a nostalgic adventure to see her again?"

I thought about it for several days, and as the intrigue grew, I said "Yes." Herman invited us to dinner at his home.

As I walked in I saw her sitting in a deep chair in a white dress, her lips quite red, her cheeks slightly rouged, and her eyes dark and smiling. When I walked to her chair she stood up and I brashly kissed her lightly on the cheek, which I could see surprised her. We got along unusually well.

Our conversational dates were filled with 1920s reminiscences, with proud exchanges about our families, and each of us, directly or indirectly, tried to find what our interests and values were now. I soon met her children and their families, and I introduced her to mine. During the years that followed we called each other several times a week and dined at least once a week, either alone or with other couples our age. We enjoyed our phone conversations, but much more our personal times together. I remained in my home, and she in her condominium. I found Adeline as lovely and genial as I remembered her when she was in her twenties. She was full of verve and love of life then and, amazingly, just as spirited today. Her children and grandchildren adore her, her many friends seek her companionship, and I marvel and love her youthful, joyous spirit. Our mutual caring for each other is continuing – I at 93 and she at 89.

The only new idea that is now bubbling in my mind is something "way out," but in a way, a visionary extension of my new spiritual thinking. It is to write a book with the title, *The Man of Tomorrow*, with the subtitle, *What will He be Like 5,000 Years from Now?* It is a fantasy, but what I like about it is that it will stretch my imagination to its outer limits. I couldn't engage in this literary luxury when I needed money, but I can afford it now. It's an enticing contemplation, and I'm already wondering what ideas will come my way.

I'm grateful at 93 to have the energy to manage my buildings, follow my spiritual quest, look toward writing *Man of Tomorrow*, be involved with my family, and enjoy quality time with Adeline. While I try to be active on all five fronts, entropy – natural degeneration – is also active. Macular degeneration, inner ear problems, and waning energy are having their say in my body. In addition, if I may use a bit of levity, many of my minor parts hurt, and those that don't hurt don't work. But I try to carry on with all my unfinished projects and interests, because I'd rather fall on my feet than fade away in bed.

However, as the natural gift of death looms before me, my present human conjectural view is that endless adventurous incarnations lie ahead in my soul's eternity; but my ultimate reliance about my destiny after death is what the Process of Creation, or God, has in store for me.

All my life I have been looking for and finding new beginnings. It should not surprise you that when the time comes, I'll be on the lookout for the ultimate new beginning – life after death.